Managing the Asian Century

Series editor
Purnendu Mandal, Texas, USA

Managing the Asian Century provides a platform for scholastic discussions and stresses the need for a holistic framework to understand Asia as an emerging economic global powerhouse. Books published in this series cover Asia-centric topics in economics, production, marketing, finance, entrepreneurship, education, culture, technology, as well as other areas of importance to Asian economics. The series will publish edited volumes based on papers submitted to international and regional conferences that focus on specific Asia-Pacific themes, such as investment in education, women's rights, entrepreneurship, climate change, wage inequality, challenges in governance, and corruption. Books in this series are of keen interest to researchers and policy planners around the world and will be used by universities for graduate and doctoral level studies.

More information about this series at http://www.springer.com/series/13579

Purnendu Mandal • John Vong
Editors

Development of Tourism and the Hospitality Industry in Southeast Asia

Springer

Editors
Purnendu Mandal
College of Business
Lamar University
Texas, USA

John Vong
Lee Kuan Yew School of Public Policy
National University of Singapore
Singapore, Singapore

ISSN 2364-5857 ISSN 2364-5865 (electronic)
Managing the Asian Century
ISBN 978-981-13-5699-5 ISBN 978-981-287-606-5 (eBook)
DOI 10.1007/978-981-287-606-5

Springer Singapore Heidelberg New York Dordrecht London

Softcover re-print of the Hardcover 1st edition 2016

Printed on acid-free paper

Springer Science+Business Media Singapore Pte Ltd. is part of Springer Science+Business Media (www.springer.com)

Preface

International tourism is rising faster, and much faster, than the global economic growth. According to the World Bank, the global economy still flounders as the high-income countries suffer from withdrawal symptoms of the past legacies of financial excess. Global growth in 2014 was 2.6 % and 2013 was even lower. But against the tide, the international tourism is doing great. In 2014 international arrivals reached 1,138 million, which is 51 million more than 2013. According to UN World Tourism Organization (UNWTO Asia Pacific Newsletter 2015, Issue 38), global tourism grew at 4.7 % in 2014; but the Asia Pacific region grew by 5 %, and this region is expected to maintain that steady growth in the future.

The UNWTO estimates that the business volume of global tourism is at least equivalent to the trade volume of oil exports, food products, or automobiles. In fact tourism has become a significant commerce pathway for many developing countries. There is little wonder that much encouragement is given by international development to embed tourism as a tool for poverty alleviation.

There is a strong belief that in the next decade, the strongest growth of tourism will come from Asia and the Americas, around 4–5 % for both regions, as per a survey of over 300 tourism experts reported by the UNWTO. It is expected that substantial growth will be driven by Asian inbound destinations and outbound source markets with China leading the way. This has something to do with the rise of the middle class with sufficient spending power. The total number of outbound travelers from China is expected to have increased to 109 million in 2014.

The International Monetary Fund (IMF) stated that the world's gross domestic product grew 3.4 % for 2014 up from 3 % in 2013. China, India, and Southeast Asia were the key drivers of this growth.

A joint study by the Singapore Tourism Board, Visa, and Mc Kinsey & Co. revealed that over the next decade, the expenditure by Gen Y Asians, those born between the early 1980s and early 2000, on international travel is expected to increase to 340 billion dollars. Incidentally the population of Gen Y Asians accounts for about a quarter of Asia's total population.

This book is written for those who want to understand the travel patterns generated in Asia, by Asia, and of Asia. Each of the articles is well-researched and succinctly articulated. It will refresh the minds of those who are steeped into the practice and research of international traveler. It will be a giant leap for those who are venturing into the subject of international tourism for the first time.

In the end we hope that the book will give credence and respectability to the study of hospitality, tourism, and travels and offer encouragement to each author whose paper is published herein.

Singapore, Singapore
TX, USA

John Vong
Purnendu Mandal

Contents

Chapter 1
Destination ASEAN, Beyond 2015

K. Thirumaran and Pamela Arumynathan

Abstract The 2015 year-end will mark a new era for the Association of Southeast Asian Nations that seeks to transform from a loosely held cooperating nations to a more closely knit "ASEAN Economic Community" (AEC) of over 600 million people. Greater economic cooperation is predicted to accelerate intra-ASEAN mobility. The AEC is expected to be characterized by the removal of tariffs and non-tariff barriers to trade, common external tariffs, and free movement of capital, goods, labor, and people. In all of ASEAN, tourism is a key economic sector that has implications for societies and cultures. This chapter evaluates the integrating elements that affect the tourism sector in member states. Building on earlier research and current tourism industry practices in ASEAN, three key areas are examined: employment and inbound and intra-ASEAN travel strategies. The implementation of the mutual recognition agreement and managed mobility of skilled labor opens up new economic vistas for people in the region seeking opportunities beyond national boundaries.

Keywords Intra-ASEAN mobility • Regional opportunity • ASEAN integration • AEC • ASEAN tourism

1.1 Introduction

The advent of the ASEAN Economic Community (AEC) on December 2015 will have an impact on labor and entrepreneurial mobility in the tourism industry. The AEC's potential is currently at a predictive stage, and various member states are at different stages of preparations. According to the blueprint, the AEC 2015 intends to "transform ASEAN into a region with free movement of goods, services, investments, skilled labor, and freer flow of capital" (Heng 2012). However, as the AEC emerges in the latter part of 2015, member countries' tourism policies indicate

K. Thirumaran, Ph.D. (✉) • P. Arumynathan, M.Ed.
JCU, Singapore, Singapore
e-mail: k.thirumaran@jcu.edu.au; pamela.arumynathan@jcu.edu.au

P. Mandal, J. Vong (eds.), *Development of Tourism and the Hospitality Industry in Southeast Asia*, Managing the Asian Century,
DOI 10.1007/978-981-287-606-5_1

counter developments at the national level, contradicting the meaning of an economic community. Nevertheless, the AEC is expected to have a positive impact on tourism. By 2020, ASEAN will draw even closer forming both a security community and sociocultural community. Together, these formations will witness new regional institutions servicing the people and consolidating local resources to a level sufficiently competitive with larger entities such as India and China (Chiangrai Times 2014).

Each year ASEAN youths gather in one of the member countries and discuss issues related to ASEAN unity and developments for young people within the region. During one such occasion, youths gathering in Myanmar in 2014 called for inclusive, grassroots economic development (Erviani 2014). ASEAN youth responses and the declarations of the annual ASEAN Youth Forum reveal aspirations for greater regional social integration and economic liberalization. The oxymoron of youth keenness and intensification of bureaucracy from 2015 presents challenges for skilled labor movements and tourism flows (Chia 2014). The leaders, on the other hand, have thus far led ASEAN as an elite consensus-seeking group with economic programs promulgated by intergovernmental ministries focusing mainly on technical exchanges in training, education, and economic cooperation.

The establishment of AEC is a significant step taken towards formalizing regional integration. The AEC is aimed to create a single production base and a single market among the member nations, and the AEC will enable ASEAN to create a highly competitive economic region. With the establishment of the AEC, the region is expected to establish an equitable economic development; the region will also be able to integrate more fully into the global economy (Destination Thailand News 2014). The AEC is expected to increase cooperation in the areas of human resource development, recognition of professional qualifications, capacity building, and all other types of macroeconomic and financial policies. The AEC will transform the ASEAN nations into a region that will enjoy free movement of goods, services, and professionals, and there will be a free flow of investment and capital. This chapter examines the state of ASEAN tourism and the AEC's potential impact on the industry in the context of promoting the destination as a single entity.

1.2 Brief Comparisons and Dynamism of ASEAN

The number of tourist arrivals into ASEAN is almost equal to the world's most popular destination, France. France received 84 million visitors in 2013 and is expected to host 100 million tourists by 2030 (France Diplomatie 2014). The European Union (EU), China, Australia, Korea, and Japan are the top five countries or regions supplying ASEAN with tourists. The ASEAN grouping's economy burgeoned to over two trillion dollars in 2013, putting it ahead of India (US$1.8 trillion) and Australia (US$1.5 trillion) (The World Bank 2014); ASEAN employs 26 million people and contributes US$96 billion dollars to the GDP. The ASEAN grouping has singled out tourism as a significant area to enhance the region's attractiveness and consolidate its dynamism to an advanced level (The World Bank 2014).

ASEAN may seem like the EU, but there are a number of differences between the two, which distinguish them from each other. With the AEC, it is yet to be seen if such open borders will become a reality by late 2015. The processes of EU's decisionmaking are very transparent; the transparency sets the ground rules for the accountability of decisionmakers. The EU has been able to bring in transparency because it has adopted formal rules and regulations via the Schengen Treaty embedded into its economic integration policy (NNT 2014a, b). However, both the EU and ASEAN have been using soft, informal, and voluntary mechanisms for bringing about regional cooperation and integration. This soft approach has helped ASEAN to achieve increased integration among member countries.

On the tourism front, ASEAN has two key websites that promote the region as a single destination (Abonyi 2012a, b) with multiple themes to encompass all the varied tourism landscapes. Thus far, ASEAN tourism efforts have been limited to familiarization tours, official training exchange programs, and website promotion for industry partners without substantial regional integration of travel initiatives or programs. In 2011, the ASEAN Secretariat released a strategic plan for tourism development in the region. Vision 2015 advocates greater connectivity and enhanced tourism product variety. The ASEAN development plan also seeks to involve residents through sustainability and responsible tourism (Wicakesena 2011). Of the broad strategies, three points are clear: to develop tourism standards with a certification process recognized by all member states, travel facilitation, and ASEAN connectivity. These approaches directly affect the tourism industry and are examined to the extent to which progress has been made towards this direction within the context of AEC.

1.3 The Challenge of ASEAN as a Single Destination

One of the biggest challenges facing AEC 2015 is to present the community as a single destination. It is not an easy task to brand the different Southeast Asian nations under a single umbrella (Heng 2012). All the countries have their unique identities; they practice cultures of their own; and the customs and traditions of each country are clearly distinguishable from the others. It is hoped that greater economic integration and heightened tourism activities will eventually impact the social well-being of the people positively. Henceforth, this chapter examines the key areas the AEC will have to negotiate to enhance the region as a single destination in relation to travel taxes, institutional barriers, and integrated regional marketing.

However, the question is whether one meaningful theme would be sufficient to identify and represent the community of states and their destinations or whether a multi-themed approach would be more appropriate. Second, can the ten nations be sold as a single destination by focusing on similarities, which the Southeast Asian nations cherish (Erviani 2014)? The nations have developed destination themes, in particular to encourage multi-country trips across the region, ranging from cuisine appreciation to tropical sports and recreation. Different taglines are used for promotional activities, such as "The tastes of Southeast Asia," "ASEAN, a tropical paradise," "World Class Cities," "Experience Diverse traditions," "Sport and relaxation," and "Diverse Contemporary Creativity." Thus far, in tourism literature, no studies have been done on the marketing and representation of conglomerations of destinations as single theme versus multi-theme touristic spaces. More research in this aspect can be enlightening on the efficiencies of different models of marketing the region.

1.3.1 Taxes and Visas

Indonesia, Thailand, and the Philippines all have departure taxes. At the borders between Singapore and Malaysia, foreign vehicles pay tolls and entry taxes. Long-term and multiple-entry visa applications also require cash payments (Erviani 2014). While ASEAN's final objective is clear in the upcoming AEC, at the time of writing, there is no indication of how these barriers would be lifted in the spirit of the ASEAN Economic Community 2015. On November 2001, at the seventh ASEAN summit, member countries signed a tourism agreement. Under the agreement, two articles called for extending visa exemption arrangements and phasing out travel levies and travel taxes on nationals of ASEAN (ASEAN 2001). Myanmar is one of the member countries that still requires a visa application for Singapore, Malaysia, and Indonesian nationals. Meanwhile, the Philippines, Myanmar, Cambodia, and Indonesia are cooperating to develop a "Smart Visa" for travelers. Aside from technical issues related to interoperability of a regional system, state security and immigration requirements remain inhibiting factors for a universal visa scheme for ASEAN.

1.3.2 Common ASEAN Tourism Curriculum

Another crucial solution to the problems and issues faced by the ASEAN community is education. Part of this educational feature is the CATC, the Common ASEAN Tourism Curriculum; it is an approved common curriculum used by tourism professionals from ASEAN nations. The CATC creates a link between the regional qualifications framework and the skills recognition system (Rivera and Danessa 2014). The concept of CATC is based on a number of other concepts, such as the Vientiane Action Plan (VAP), ASEAN Tourism Agreement (ATA), and the Roadmap for Integration of Tourism Sector (RITS). The CATC is a well-structured, flexible, and industry-based curriculum; it is designed to meet the varying needs and requirements of the member nations. The curriculum focuses on the competencies that have been adopted by all the member nations of ASEAN. The framework of the curriculum is industry based and includes vocations such as front office, housekeeping, food production, food and beverage service, travel agencies, and tour operations.

Although a number of initiatives were taken for the marketing of tourism in the region and the promotion of intraregional activities among member states, little has been done to understand and address hindrances to cooperation. In a region spurred by economic growth, the rising middle class of 600 million people is significant in itself in terms of ASEAN's domestic and intraregional travel markets (Wicakesena 2011). The diversity of tropical Southeast Asia offers a rich palette of colors and tastes to tourists. From history, culture, and nature to shopping, spas, and luxury holidays, all of these and more are available in a region that is predominately peaceful and stable.

1.3.3 Education and Standardization

With the advent of AEC, the concept of ASEAN's Mutual Recognition Arrangement on Tourism Professionals will also come into force. The MRA-TP is a concept that has been designed to facilitate movement of skilled tourism professionals among member states. These tourism professionals can join tourism companies in any of the ASEAN member nations.

Unification of the industry allows the creation of benchmarks and provides for training and qualifications recognized across the boundaries of member states. The competency standards for tourism professionals have already been worked out with graduates able to have their certifications and competencies recognized across borders. For example, a general, branch, or travel manager has to possess eleven functional competencies. These include the ability to manage financial operations, develop and implement a business plan, and organize and coordinate meetings. It is very important for the AEC to ensure that all of its education policies, systems, and institutions are serving all the requirements of the business (Abonyi 2012a, b). In order to fulfill that need, the community needs to continuously provide its members with intensive training sessions, particularly in the area of management and leadership.

1.3.4 Travel Entities Cooperation and Collaboration

Travel agents, tour operators, and transport companies in the region also need to come up with smart programs to keep in step with the goal of the AEC's approach to tourism – to make the Southeast Asian region a seamless travel escape. To accomplish this, the airlines could standardized pricing or offer an ASEAN regional ticket at a particular price. With this ticket, passengers can fly to all the capitals or regional cities of each country without having to pay for each segment – much like an around the world ticket.

Websites such as ASEANTA (the ASEAN Tourism Association (http://aseanta.org/)) and ASEAN Tourism (http://www.aseantourism.travel/welcome) and many other affiliated organizations should realign and restructure the positioning of products and services holistically. Specific destinations and attractions could continue to be highlighted as distinct segments of the travel experience but within a more holistic framework of ASEAN. Formed in 1971, ASEANTA comprises public and private organizations from member states coming together to address issues related to the tourism industry with the ASEAN governments and implement efforts to promote intra-ASEAN tourism. The ASEAN Tourism website is the official site of ASEAN that promotes the various destinations. It contains more information of the various destinations and tour programs in ASEAN. In the same vein, a new research-consultancy organization comprising of academics has registered their intention to affiliate with ASEAN as the ASEAN Tourism Research Association (ATRA). Together, these three highlighted entities reflect serious efforts and interests in the region to consolidate and enhance the tourism resources to serve the people and region.

1.4 Preparations and Movements in Anticipation of AEC 2015

In anticipation of the opportunities, many businesses and individuals are hedging their bets in some instances, and in other cases, whole communities or countries are insulating themselves from the easy movement of people. For example, taking advantage of the developments, Cebu Pacific and AirAsia are repositioning themselves in the frontiers of intra-ASEAN passenger travel (Rivera and Danessa 2014). Cebu Pacific, for example, has plans to purchase over 50 short-haul planes and to map out a regional strategy that would leverage on the flow of people from within.

Similarly, AirAsia is continuing to garner partnership with destinations outside the region and to feeder service its existing flights within the region (NNT 2014a, b). Therefore, ASEAN's open skies would alleviate government objections other than meeting aviation standards and local airport taxes. The latter is a matter that has not clearly been addressed in the ASEAN blueprint. If those landing rights taxes and passenger taxes were lifted with the exception of airport services taxes, it would then be understandable and acceptable in the new AEC 2015 configuration. Therefore, airlines in the industry have to continue working with ASEAN governments in relation to airport taxes, rights, and handling fees that are beneficially frameworked and delinked from the interests of national competitiveness.

The AEC 2015 is also about ASEAN citizens traveling within the member states to settle down among locals as new residents and compete for employment opportunities. It is expected that young people might find it lucrative to work in a more prosperous city or where the exchange rate is of higher yield vis-à-vis to their own country's currency (Chia 2014). The attractiveness of Thailand, Malaysia, and Singapore might lead to a movement of professionals from Vietnam, Cambodia, and Indonesia. For example, a Vietnamese or Thai citizen can choose to stay in Bali and seek to work in the tourism industry there. In addition, given such possibilities, their residency and involvement in the communities will inevitably have an impact on the local residents and the community as a whole. Bali's Grand Council of Customary Villages (MUDP) most recently conducted a SWOT analysis to ensure that Balinese culture remains intact when citizens of ASEAN start to settle in Bali for jobs or business opportunities (Erviani 2014). Bali, for example, has taken action by passing a community law (Heng 2012). This law preserves the decisionmaking at the village level on matters such as land, properties, and religious celebrations as solely the constitutional rights of Balinese only.

The Thais are also fully conscious of the potential tourism factor in the AEC. In this respect, Chiang Mai International Airport is poised to play an important regional corridor hub to Indochina, India, and China. The Thais through Bangkok Airways have already developed a strong network of modern cities such as Phuket, Udon Thani, Mandalay, and Yangon (Destination Thailand 2014). Another example of Thailand's full preparedness is the fact that the Chiang Mai zoo refurbished its prayer rooms in anticipation of AEC channeling more Muslim travelers to Thailand (NNT 2014a, b). Cebu Pacific on the other hand is expected to receive 43 aircrafts adding to its existing 50 aircraft fleet between 2014 and 2021. That will allow it to compete in an AEC open skies policy with the more established and highly partnered and networked Malaysian budget carrier AirAsia that has over 120 aircrafts (Rivera 2014). This prepositioning within the industry suggests a real interest in maintaining a degree of national as well as industry competitiveness. While it has to be competitive between the major players, the regional framework should also examine ways where cooperation can benefit to promote the AEC as a key destination.

1.5 The Leaders in AEC Tourism

There are a number of geopolitical factors that can be taken as a competitive edge by the ASEAN members. The regional grouping's informal ways of cooperation and consensus seeking on major issues have thus far helped the members to create a sense of confidence and trust rather than just building a relationship with legalistic structures and styles (Wicakesena 2011). The ASEAN members have faced pressures from various external developments for the increased levels of economic integration so that the member nations can compete in the global markets and investments.

Tourism is one of the very few industries in the world that has the greatest multiplier effects. The industry consumes a wide range of local goods and services which becomes a reason for the wide distribution of income (Chia 2014). The industry also enjoys a very high number of positive spillovers. According to the surveys of the World Trade Organization (WTO) and the World Travel and Tourism Council (WTTC), for every job created in the tourism industry, there are more than five jobs created as a result of that first job. It is not just the economic benefits that can be achieved but a strong tourism industry can act as a mechanism for social change. It can be a reason for the incorporation of new and innovative ideas and values.

In the lead to a regional economic community, Thailand and the Philippines appear to be in the forefront of taking the region to the next level (Destination Thailand News 2014). Thailand, for example, is the only country that has started the AEC tourism Thailand website, http://en.aectourismthai.com/, long before other member states, suggesting its leadership role in the AEC tourism (Destination Thailand News 2014). The website promotes the region and explains the AEC. The website highlights news about AEC activities and progress, exchange rates, destination videos, and informative links. Under the ASEAN Dream Destinations, the Thais have taken the lead to conduct a competition of pictures and videos with a hashtag.

Additionally, on September 2014, Thailand inaugurated a human resources development institution primarily for the spa and massage industry to bring up-to-date international standards for Thai massage and spa therapists (NNT 2014a, b). With this institution, Thailand hopes to maintain its lead in the spa tourism while at the same time providing young therapists opportunities of employment or entrepreneurship in other ASEAN member states (Destination Thailand News 2014). In most places in Thai cities including at the very micro level, one could see some forms of AEC regional integration promotion. One such example is a motorized taxi, tuk-tuk, with a banner sticker on the back of the driver's seat that reads: "Welcome to ASEAN 2015." Thailand is also aware of its people's spoken English level and has targeted schools to raise the quality of spoken English and emphasized the importance of knowledge about ASEAN (City News 2013) which does not seem like a key endeavor in many other member states (Destination Thailand News 2014).

In almost all the hospitality businesses in Singapore and in some instances in Malaysia and Thailand, one will see a Filipino staff. This might be because of the English proficiency in the Philippines compared to other Asian cities. The Filipino accent is relaxed and neutral (Erviani 2014). The fact the Filipinos have good speaking and social skills makes them competitive for jobs in the industry. Many young Filipinos can learn a foreign language fast, e.g., Mandarin, which is widely spoken in Singapore and other Asian cities such as Macau and Hong Kong (Heng 2012). Being bilingual or multilingual gives these young Filipinos an edge to work in the hospitality and gaming industry where both English and Mandarin are popularly used. Some young Filipinos might prefer to stay and work in Manila due to these developments; however, some others might travel and move out of the country due to the still strong Singapore dollar, for instance, as compared to the Philippine peso.

1.6 Conclusion

Earlier we viewed AEC 2015 as a drive towards harnessing the resources of over 600 million people for the purpose of creating a common market within the context of the rise of India and China. The most important element lacking in the blueprint thus far is creating a belief in ASEAN Economic Community as a social unit of brotherhood bringing people together at noneconomic levels of viewing the community of member states as a group of family and seeing each other as part of a common destiny. In this way, when moving towards the military and sociocultural community in 2020, there would be foundations laid for greater citizenry participation, cohesiveness, and enhanced respectful cooperation. More can be done in AEC other than the already envisaged infrastructure connectivity and visa-free travel for individuals from member states as well as a common visa program for noncitizens of ASEAN. Three areas that can possibly be improved upon as a community of nations are in the area of aviation travel ticketing, industry exchanges, and attractions. There needs to be a creation of common institutions and laws that can ensure the enforcement of the agreements and contracts among the member states. Establishment of such institutions has been acknowledged as a goal and mechanism for regional integration.

Indeed, ASEAN members would face challenges with the setup of AEC; however, this cannot overrule the advantages or the competitive edges that the ASEAN member nations enjoy. The member states are strategically located in the geographical region of Asia that is dynamic; the region is facing sound macroeconomic fundamentals and is going through an economic growth phase (Heng 2012). The productive capabilities of these Southeast Asian states are also very high and are considered a hub to foreign direct investments. Additionally, ASEAN member states possess high historical and cultural backgrounds, and this is a very strong point that can be optimized by the travel community of member nations.

At the aviation trade level, ASEAN could come up with programs for both domestic and international travelers for a special ticket that would entitle them to all ten countries in their respective carriers or just simply in a selected national carrier of ASEAN. This suggested scheme is similar to an around the world ticket offered by many airlines internationally. Another project ASEAN can adopt is the institutional exchanges for training and education in tourism, a trainee or internship program that cuts through the red tape of individual state requirements.

Non-archetype tours are available elsewhere. Instead of focusing on a single theme such as resort vacations like much of the Caribbean, Southeast Asia has more to offer as depicted in multi-theme promotions. However, more needs to be done in terms of industry partnerships, entrepreneurs finding opportunities in these disconnected themes, travel agents, tour operators, and national and regional frameworks. One example is ATRA, a newly formed organization, which aims to promote regional university-level cooperation in research and consultancy works in ASEAN. This alliance formation of ten universities includes universities both internal and external to the region such as Taylor's University (Malaysia), Royal University of Phnom Penh (Cambodia), Bandung Institute of Tourism (Indonesia), Laos National Institute of Tourism and Hospitality (Laos), Lyceum of the Philippines and University of the Philippines (Philippines), Prince Songkla (Thailand), and Hoa Sen University (Vietnam). Leveraging the intellectual circles of the tourism industry would further produce higher levels of practical solutions to the industry and community.

While most ordinary citizens may not understand or be aware of AEC 2015, it is telling how the governments have carefully orchestrated this move to integrate member states economically, later socially, and militarily. A survey conducted in Indonesia suggested that 80 % did not know about the AEC though more importantly upon receiving an explanation, they agreed with the idea of integration.

The lack of knowledge among the locals of the AEC 2015 could be due to the government's failure to socialize and explain the concept of the AEC to the public. The idea of the AEC might be elitist and state centric and designed without involving public participation. The public might also see little relevance between the potential benefits that the AEC could provide in their day-to-day lives. Therefore, for aspiring ASEAN citizens, there are possible employment opportunities with those holding qualified and certified skills in other member states as well as niches in tourism in the more growing economies of Cambodia, Laos, and Myanmar.

In the age of global economic alliances, it has become a necessity for smaller countries to unite with other regional trading partners to form a larger consortium. Through the Community Progress Monitoring System, the ASEAN Secretariat is set to monitor the progress of the AEC and the implementation of the project of various projects. However, in order to achieve success, national sacrifices and short-term structural changes are often required. According to Max Weber (1994), the rules and regulations of bureaucracy entrap individuals in an "iron cage" limiting movement and aspirations. The standardization of credentials and services in a consolidated ASEAN tourism industry also reflects the bureaucratic process of McDonaldization identified by Ritzer (2008). In order to achieve the aspirations of young people of the ten member group of ASEAN, free movement of people and labor in the AEC must be real and substantial. Then only the AEC at the grassroots level will share the same fervor as the elites and political leadership in the eventual formation of a security and sociocultural community in 2020.

References

Abonyi G (2012a) The emerging ASEAN Economic Community (AEC 2015) in the wider regional and global economy–a macro view (Part 1). Retrieved from https://www.maxwell.syr.edu/uploadedFiles/exed/sites/asiapolicy/Emerging%20ASEAN%20Economic_Brief_Abonyi.pdf

Abonyi G (2012b) The emerging ASEAN Economic Community (AEC 2015) and the challenge of innovation-micro view (Part 2). Asia Policy Briefs, June, 1–10. Retrieved from https://maxwell.syr.edu/uploadedFiles/exed/sites/asiapolicy/FINAL%20-%20June%20-%20GA%20Brief%202%20-%20(Micro)%20Innovation%20and%20Emerging%20ASEAN%20Economic%20Community%20LS%20markup.pdf

ASEAN (2001) ASEAN tourism agreement. Retrieved from http://www.asean.org/communities/asean-economic-community/item/asean-tourism-agreement-2

Chia SY (2014) Towards freer movement of skilled labour in AEC 2015 and beyond (No. PB-2014-02). Retrieved from http://www.eria.org/ERIA-PB-2014-02.pdf

Chiangrai Times (2014) Chiang Rai and other gateway provinces see jump in land prices ahead of AEC, 16 August. Retrieved from http://www.chiangraitimes.com/chiang-rai-and-other-gateway-provinces-see-jump-in-land-prices-ahead-of-aec.html

City News Chiang Mai (2013) ASEAN, the AEC, 2015…What's all the fuss about?? 1 Aug. Retrieved from http://chiangmaicitynews.com/blog.php?id=2150

Destination Thailand News (2014) Bangkok airways welcomes AEC with four new routes from Chiang Mai, 31 October. Retrieved from http://destinationthailandnews.com/transportation/aviation/bangkok-airways-welcomes-aec-4-new-routes-chiang-mai-2.html
Erviani NK (2014) Village council gears up for new era, 7 August. The Jakarta Post. Retrieved from http://www.thejakartapost.com/news/2014/08/07/village-council-gears-new-era.html
France Diplomatie (2014) Statistics on tourism for 2013 (July 2014). Retrieved on 18 Dec 2014 from http://www.diplomatie.gouv.fr/en/french-foreign-policy-1/tourism/the-place-of-tourism-in-the-french/article/statistics-on-tourism-for-2013-07
Heng PK (2012) ASEAN integration in 2030: United States perspectives. Retrieved from http://papers.ssrn.com/sol3/papers.cfm?abstract_id=2101537
NNT (2014a). Chiang Mai opens institution to train spa and massage therapists for AEC, 14 Sept 2014. Retrieved from http://thainews.prd.go.th/centerweb/newsen/NewsDetail?NT01_NewsID=WNECO5709140010004
NNT (2014b) Chiang Mai Zoo renovates muslim prayer rooms for AEC integration, 13 August. Retrieved from http://www.pattayamail.com/news/chiang-mai-zoo-renovates-muslim-prayer-rooms-for-aec-integration-40330
Ritzer G (2008) The McDonaldization of society. Pine Forge Press, London
Rivera DO (2014) Cebu pacific sees more opportunities in new routes under ASEAN single market., 6 August. Retrieved from http://www.gmanetwork.com/news/story/373676/economy/companies/cebu-pacific-sees-more-opportunities-in-new-routes-under-ASEAN-single-market
The World Bank (2014) World DataBank – world development indicators. Accessed 18 Aug 2014. http://databank.worldbank.org/data/views/reports/tableview.aspx?isshared=true
Weber M (1994) Political writings. In: Lassman P (ed) Cambridge texts in the history of political thought, Trans. Ronald Speirs, vii. Cambridge University Press, Cambridge
Wicakesena B (2011) The readiness of Indonesians towards the 2015 ASEAN economic community: a review, 28 July. Go Live Indonesia. Retrieved from http://goliveindonesia.com/2011/07/28/the-readiness-of-indonesians-towards-the-2015-ASEAN-economic-community-a-review/

K. Thirumaran Over the past 5 years, Dr. Thirumaran's research focus has been on Singapore, Bali, Malaysia, Bhutan and studies on Chinese and Indian tourists. He has contributed articles in edited books, journal, encyclopedia, and newspapers. Dr. Thirumaran is a frequent guest lecturer in special interest tourism and civic education at public schools in Singapore. His teaching style provides many opportunities beyond classroom learning for students to undertake fieldwork and forge connections with the travel and hospitality industry.

Pamela Arumynathan With over 18 years of experience in the field of education, exposed to the nuances and subtleties of the process of language acquisition and teaching to a variety of international students, Ms Arumynathan has come not only to enjoy her profession as an educator but also to execute it with the highest level of professionalism and passion. She believes in giving students ownership of their learning. Ms Arumynathan is also responsible for formulating language acquisition training materials and conducting workshops and classes for hospitals and various associations.

Chapter 2
Factors Affecting Willingness of Foreign Tourists to Spend Money in Benefiting Local People

I Gusti Ayu Oka Suryawardani, Agung Suryawan Wiranatha, and Christine Petr

Abstract Bali has been known as one of the most popular tourist destinations in the world due to its cultural activities and natural scenery. Tourism has now become a driving force in the economic development of Bali Province and has become the leading economic sector in Bali's economy. Assessing foreign tourists' familiarity, satisfaction, motivation and perceptions of a destination regarding foreign tourists' visit is really important as these aspects affect human behaviour which provide suggestions for increasing level of desire to learn, improve experience and enjoy activities effectively which leads people to choose and pursue certain goals when travelling. How to motivate and hold visitors' attention throughout revisit is also important.

This chapter examines opinion of foreign tourists on accommodation and restaurant services, expectation and satisfaction level on whole trips, emotional experience and level of agreement on spending money to benefit Balinese people. The chapter also analyses relationship between variables, i.e. relationship between satisfaction, familiarity, motivation and perceptions of foreign tourists regarding the quality of products and services in Bali's tourism and their willingness to spend money to benefit the Balinese people. A survey was undertaken in Bali on 600 foreign tourists. The results indicate that tourists who visit Bali are willing to spend money on local people and be a part of the system of Bali tourism in terms of maintaining sustainable tourism. Most of tourists are also willing to stay in villages and prefer authenticity of local products. Foreigners prefer to stay in locally decorated Balinese style facilities and are willing to give more money to be used for environmental

I.G.A.O. Suryawardani (✉) • A.S. Wiranatha
Udayana University, Denpasar, Indonesia
e-mail: gungdani@gmail.com; balitruly@yahoo.com

C. Petr
EIREST, Sorbonne Universitė Paris 1, Paris, France
e-mail: drchpetr@gmail.com

P. Mandal, J. Vong (eds.), *Development of Tourism and the Hospitality Industry in Southeast Asia*, Managing the Asian Century,
DOI 10.1007/978-981-287-606-5_2

protection in order to minimise negative impacts of tourism development in Bali as long as the mechanism is well organised. They would also love to live with the harmonious interaction with local Balinese people and willing to maintain cultural heritage of Bali.

Keywords Authenticity • Local products • Benefit local people • Sustainable tourism • Bali

2.1 Introduction

Although foreign tourists are still interested in visiting Bali which is one of the destinations in the world, the emergence of new holiday destinations that offer lower prices and, in some cases, higher-quality facilities cannot be avoided, such as Thailand, Malaysia, Singapore and other countries which have similar culture of Bali. Attempts have been carried out by the government and the tourism industry to promote the destination and improve services, hospitality and infrastructure; however, further efforts need to be undertaken. Quality and satisfaction of tourists cannot be separated as Swarbrooke and Horner (2009) say that the quality is the determinant in achieving tourist satisfaction, and satisfaction of tourists will form the tourist loyalty. They also said that complaint handling and tourists' trust also affect tourist loyalty since more variables and their interactions can be taken into account.

The study of consumer perception, satisfaction, expectation and loyalty on a destination has been pointed out in the marketing literature as one of the major driving forces in the new marketing era (Brodie et al. 1997); the analysis and exploration of this concept is relatively recent in tourism research. Some studies recognise that understanding which factors increase tourist loyalty is valuable information for tourism marketers and managers (Flavian et al. 2001). Many destinations rely strongly on repeat visitation because it is less expensive to retain repeat tourists than to attract new ones (Um et al. 2006). In addition, Baker and Crompton (2000) show that the strong link between consumer loyalty and profitability is a reality in the tourism industry. The study of the influential factors of destination loyalty is not new to tourism research. Some studies show that the revisit intention is explained by the number of previous visits (Mazursky 1989; Court and Lupton 1997; Petrick et al. 2001). Besides destination familiarity, the overall satisfaction that tourists experience for a particular destination is also regarded as a predictor of the tourist's intention to prefer the same destination again (Oh 1999; Kozak and Rimmington 2000; Bowen 2001; Alexandros and Shabbar 2005; Bigné et al. 2005).

Other studies propose more comprehensive frameworks. Bigné et al. (2001) developed a model of return intentions to Spanish destinations through destination image, perceived quality and satisfaction as explanatory variables. Yoon and Uysal (2005) use tourist satisfaction as a moderator construct between motivations and tourist loyalty. Furthermore, Um et al. (2006) proposed a model based on revisiting intentions that establishes satisfaction as both a predictor of revisiting intentions and as a moderator variable between constructs and perceived attractiveness, perceived quality of service and perceived value for money. More complex models have the advantage of allowing a better understanding of tourist behaviour since more variables and their interactions can be taken into account.

In order to study the factors affecting foreign tourists in Bali, a survey was undertaken during the period of April to June 2013 in four main destinations in Bali, i.e. Kuta, Nusa Dua, Sanur and Ubud. The study focused mainly on the assessment of willingness of foreign tourists to participate in the development of Bali's tourism.

2.2 Tourism Literature

2.2.1 The Complexity of Consumer Behaviour in Travelling

Tourist plays an important role in increasing the popularity of a destination. Tourist behaviour in choosing a destination has a significant relationship to perception of tourists to destination (Goodrich 1978; Solomon 1999; Andriotis 2005). Mechanisms in forming interaction between tourists and destinations play an important role in creating a relationship between tourists and destinations. Perceptions and preferences are widely used in social research, especially in consumer behaviour, such as the study by Solomon (1999) which says that perception is one of the psychological factors that are closely related to the sensory system that plays an important role in influencing decision-making. This response is an important part of the emotional aspects of the interaction of consumers towards products. Moreover, Solomon (1999) defined perception as a process that occurs in the mind of consumer where the sensation is selected, organised and interpreted, while preference is a further expression of the perception which is expressed in an action based on choice and consumer interest. Action will be taken after going through a long process in the minds of consumers, as expressed in the following quote:

> ...Perception is process that works in mind by which sensations are selected, organized and interpreted while preferences are further expression of perception. Preference represents people/customer choices, their interest, like or dislike. Action will be taken after long process in customers' mind .... (Solomon 1999)

Meanwhile, Waite and Hawker (2009) define perception as:

> ... The ability to see, hear or be aware of something that express a particular understanding as a process of perceiving.... (Waite and Hawker 2009: 26)

Solomon (1999) adds that factors influencing preference of consumers are consumer insight about products or services, income, tastes or interests of consumers, culture and previous experience in consuming products and services. This opinion is supported by Kim and Jamal (2007) who state that the perception is the process by which a person chooses, organises and interprets information to create a picture of what is seen and felt. Solomon (1999) explains that the barrier to receive marketing messages occurs as a result of the limitations of the brain to process information, so that consumers are very selective about what they watch.

Another study by Davis (2003) found that in the summer, visitors have a different orientation in the tour. Some visitors concerned with physical attraction prefer outdoor sensations such as beach, landscape, cultural attractions and entertainment. Other groups tend to focus on exploring the environment and culture. It is suggested in his study that the process of innovation in the tourism industry should be focused on better mechanisms to manage a destination. Oh (1999) evaluates the service quality, customer satisfaction and loyalty that the holistic management model must be applied in destination management. Understanding the consumer decision-making process which focuses on customer value as a variable that is very important because of its strength rests on the perception and selection on quality customer service and customer satisfaction. It also said that the quality of service can be a mediator between perception and customer choice.

Andriotis (2005) conducted a study on the perceptions and preferences of the community in the development of tourism to boost local economies. The goal is to determine whether the entrepreneur in the field of tourism and the local population has a positive dependence on tourism development. Benchmarks used in these studies are public perception as a guide in the development of future tourism. The results showed that the perceptions and preferences of the public in the area of tourism to boost the economy are really important. Three groups expressed their perceptions exist at high levels positively to the development of tourism, although there are some differences in their agreements relating to the type and origin of tourists, facilities and management models that are considered beneficial to the area.

Goodrich (1978) conducted a study on the relationship between perceptions and preferences on a destination. Studies demonstrate how the choice of a tourist destination depends on the perception of the fun of these destinations. The results showed that the higher the score, the higher the perception of choice for the destination. The implication of this study is associated with the marketing of a destination, where stakeholders should seek to develop a positive image of a destination in order to improve the tourist choice of areas that became a tourist destination. Another implication is that the diagnosis of strengths and weaknesses on attributes relevant tourism is very helpful in making changes specifically related to the facilities and services in a destination.

Lin et al. (2012) say that recreation is a very interesting pastime and activity that improves the quality of life. In modern society, sports are very important to improve the experience of different cultures and lifestyles as a form of appreciation for the economic prosperity and progress in the field of technology. Factors that affect tourist arrivals to a destination are a traveller motif, features of a destination, distance to destination and tourist perceptions of a destination. A study on the relationship between consumer behaviour and marketing in an amusement park in Taiwan concluded that consumer behaviour has a positive correlation to the perception of tourists in the marketing mix (marketing mix) at the amusement park. Evaluation before making a visit has a positive relationship to the price. The highest relationship found in the price and place. Amongst the demographic variables, sex (gender) has a significant impact on consumer choice based on security, comfort and price level. Age and area of residence have a significant relationship to consumer choice on pricing strategies and marketing activities. This study suggests that attention to market segments based on age, sex and area of residence is important in marketing strategy for a tourist attraction.

2.2.2 *Determinants of Tourist Satisfaction on Destination*

Personal characteristics of tourists, such as perception, motivations and socio-demographic characteristics, play an important role in explaining their future behaviour. The concept of satisfaction has been recognised as one of the more important indicators of success in the marketing literature (La Barbara and Mazursky 1983; Turnbull and Wilson 1989; Pine et al. 1995; Bauer et al. 2002). Hallowell (1996) provides evidence on the connection between satisfaction, loyalty and profitability. The author refers that working with loyal customers reduces customer recruitment costs, customer price sensitivity and servicing costs. In terms of traditional marketing of products and services, loyalty can be measured by repeated sales or by recommendation to other consumers (Pine et al. 1995). Yoon and Uysal (2005) emphasise that travel destinations can also be perceived as a product which can be resold (revisited) and recommended to others (friends and family who are potential tourists). In his study about the desirability of loyal tourists, Petrick (2004) states that loyal visitors can be less price sensitive than first-time visitors. This study shows that few loyal tourists and those visiting the destination for the first time tend to spend more money during the visit.

Determining factors of satisfaction have been studied in the marketing literatures. Satisfaction can be used as a measure to evaluate the products and services offered at the destination (Ross and Iso-Ahola 1991; Noe and Uysal 1997; Bramwell 1998; Schofield 2000). Baker and Crompton (2000) define satisfaction as the tourist's emotional state after experiencing the trip. Therefore, evaluating satisfaction in terms of a travelling experience is a post-consumption process (Fornell 1992). Assessing satisfaction can help managers to improve services (Fornell 1992) and to compare organisations and destinations in terms of performance (Kotler 1993). In addition, the ability of managing feedback received from customers can be an important source of competitive advantage (Petrick et al. 2001).

Bitner (1990), Dick and Basu (1994) and Oliver (1999) show that satisfaction from products or services affects consumer loyalty. Flavian et al. (2001) add that loyalty to a product or service is not the result of the absence of alternative offers. Instead, loyalty occurs because consumers increasingly have less free time available and therefore try to simplify their buying decision process by acquiring familiar products or services. As referred above, research shows that the satisfaction that tourists experience in a specific destination is a determinant of the tourist revisiting. Furthermore, more holistic model has been used by Yoon and Uysal (2005)to explain destination loyalty in tourism research. They developed a model which relates destination loyalty with travel satisfaction and holiday motivations. This study found a significant cause-effect relationship between travel satisfaction and destination loyalty as well as between motivations and travel satisfaction.

Oh (1999) establishes service quality, perceived price, customer value and perceptions of company performance as determinants of customer satisfaction which, in turn, are used to explain revisit intentions. Bigne et al. (2001) identify that returning intentions and recommending intentions are influenced by tourism image and quality variables of the destination. Kozak and Rimmington (2000) model intends to revisit the following explanatory variables: overall satisfaction, number of previous visits and perceived performance of destination. Meanwhile, Um et al. (2006) propose a structural equation model that explains revisiting intentions as determined by satisfaction, perceived attractiveness, perceived quality of service and perceived value for money. In this study repeat visits are determined more by perceived attractiveness than by overall satisfaction. Another important conclusion from the study carried out by Um et al. (2006) is that the revisit decision-making process should be modelled in the same way as modelling a destination choice process. This implies that the personal characteristics of tourists, such as perception, motivations and socio-demographic characteristics, play an important role in explaining their future behaviour.

2.2.2.1 Perception

Perception is defined as the ability to see, hear or be aware of something that expresses a particular understanding as a process of perceiving (Waite and Hawker 2009). Perception is also defined as ‘the process by which these sensations are selected, organized and interpreted, while sensation refers to the immediate response of our sensory receptors: eyes, ears, nose, mouth and fingers to basic stimuli such as light, colour, sound, odors and textures’ (Solomon 1999:43). There are limitations in the brain’s ability to process information, so that people are very selective about what they pay attention to (called ‘perceptual vigilance’). Therefore, people practise a form of ‘psychic economy’, picking and choosing amongst stimuli to avoid being overwhelmed (Solomon 1999). The people are more likely to be aware of stimuli that are related to their current needs. Moreover, people see what they want to see and don’t see what they don’t want to see (called ‘perceptual defence’). The degree to which consumers continue to notice stimulus over time is known as ‘adaptation’ (Reisinger 2009). The process of adaptation occurs when consumers no longer pay attention to a stimulus because it is so familiar. A consumer can become habituated and require increasingly stronger ‘doses’ of a stimulus for it to be noticed. Several factors can lead to adaptation, namely, intensity, duration, discrimination, exposure and relevance. ‘Intensity’ means that less intense stimuli are less likely to be noticed. ‘Duration’ refers to the length of exposure to the stimulus; stimuli that require a relatively lengthy exposure time in order to be processed tend to habituate because they require a long attention span. 'Discrimination' relates to simple stimuli that tend to habituate because they do not require attention to detail. 'Exposure' refers to the frequency of exposure; frequently encountered stimuli tend to habituate as the rate of exposure increases. Perception is one of the social and psychological factors which, together with other factors such as personality, learning, motives and attitudes, plays an important role in influencing a person's travel decisions. In this study, these concepts of perception are adapted to obtain tourists' opinions about certain imported and local products and services in Bali (Kim and Jamal 2007).

2.2.2.2 Motivation

Despite sharing equal degrees of satisfaction, tourists with different personal features can report heterogeneous behaviours in terms of their loyalty to a destination (Mittal and Kamakura 2001). Motivation is defined as ' ... reasons for acting or behaving in a particular way toward attaining a goal ...' (Khan 1991). As a basic psychological feature, motivation stimulates an organism to act towards a desired goal and controls and sustains a certain goal. It can be considered as a driving force which psychologically reinforces an action towards a desired goal (Bashar 2010). Motivation is an internal factor that leads people to choose and pursue certain goals and experiences (Higgins et al. 2003). Meanwhile, motivation provides suggestions for increasing level of desire to learn effectively including interest, attention, relevance, confidence and satisfaction (Allesi and Trollip 1991). In this study, motivation related to reasons to visit Bali as a destination consists of vacation, visiting friends and relatives (VFR), office task, MICE (meeting, incentive, conference and exhibition), business, religion, education/research, health/beauty and sport.

Motivations form the basis of the travel decision process and therefore should also be considered when analysing destination loyalty intentions. Beerli and Martín (2004) propose that 'motivation is the need that drives an individual to act in a certain way to achieve the desired satisfaction' (Beerli and Martín 2004:626). Motivations can be intrinsic (push) or extrinsic (pull). Push motivations correspond to a tourist's desire and emotional frame of mind. Pull motivations represent the attributes of the destination to be visited. Yoon and Uysal (2005) take tourist satisfaction to be a mediator variable between motivations (pull and push) and destination loyalty. The effect of socio-demographic variables in the tourist's decision process is also an issue which has received some attention. Some studies propose that age and level of education influence the choice of destination (Woodside and Lysonski 1989; Weaver et al. 1994; Zimmer et al. 1995). Font (2000) shows that age, educational level, nationality and occupation represent factors of motivation to travel.

Oliver (1999) states that loyalty is a construct that can be conceptualised by several perspectives. Homburg and Giering (2001) measure the construct 'future behavioural intention' by using two indicators: the intention of repurchase and the intention to provide positive recommendations. In tourism research, similar approach is adopted and tourist loyalty intention is represented in terms of the intention to revisit the destination and the willingness to recommend it to friends and relatives (Oppermann 2000; Bigné et al. 2001; Chen and Gursoy 2001; Cai et al. 2003; Niininen et al. 2004; Petrick 2001). Therefore, two indicators, 'revisiting intention' and 'willingness to recommend', are used as measures of destination loyalty intention.

2.2.2.3 Familiarity

Familiarity is a quality or condition for being familiar which is classified into spatial proximity and expertise of the country (Bashar 2010). Spatial proximity describes proximity to an area, while country expertise is the accumulation of a person's experience of the quality of a destination. In this study, familiarity is related to the satisfaction of tourists during their visit in Bali. It was based on 'country of residence' (F1) which covers five continents, namely, Europe, America, Australia, Africa and Asia, while 'large code of residence' (F2) denotes the residential areas where they live, namely, Old Europe, North Europe, East Europe, South Europe, the USA, South America, Africa and Saudi Arabia, Australia, Asia and Indonesia. Meanwhile, country expertise is the accumulation of experience of the quality of a destination (Bashar 2010). In this study, it is measured in terms of 'periodicity' in visiting Bali (F3) and 'visit more than 5 times' (F4). All of the above variables influence people's travel choices (Reisinger 2009). The emotional experience of foreign tourists is one of the indicators which can be used to assess their level of satisfaction during their visit. Previous experience influences people's decision to revisit a destination (Mill and Morrison 2009). This kind of experience was also assessed in this research.

2.2.2.4 Expectation

Expectation is a cognitive process of motivation which is based on the idea that people believe there are relationships between the effort they have made, the performance they achieve and the rewards they receive from their effort and performance. People will be motivated if they believe that strong effort will lead to good performance, and good performance will lead to desired rewards (Lunenborg 2011). Expectancy theory is based on four assumptions (Pinder 1987). The first assumption is that people join organisations with expectations about their needs, motivations and past experiences. These influence how individuals react to the organisation or activities. The second assumption is that an individual's behaviour is a result of conscious choice which means that people are free to choose those behaviours suggested by their own expectancy calculations. The third assumption is that people want different things from the organisation (experience, good salary, job security, advancement and challenge), and the fourth assumption is that people will choose amongst alternatives to optimise outcomes for them personally. The expectancy theory based on these assumptions has three key elements, namely, expectancy, instrumentality and valence. A person is motivated to the degree that he or she believes that effort will lead to acceptable performance. Performance will be rewarded and the value of the rewards is highly positive (Pinder 1987). In this chapter, expectation relates to fulfilment of foreign tourists expectations regarding the whole trips in Bali.

2.2.3 *Benefit of Tourism for Local People*

According to UNWTO (2007), sustainable tourism development refers to the economic, environmental and socio-cultural aspects of tourism development, and a suitable balance must be established between these three dimensions to guarantee its long-term sustainability called 'triple bottom line'. In addition, sustainable tourism should also maintain a high level of tourist satisfaction and ensure a meaningful experience for the tourists, raising their awareness about sustainability issues and promoting sustainable tourism practices amongst them. Sustainable tourism is also defined as holistic systems that meet the need of present tourists and host regions while protecting and enhancing opportunities for the future. It is envisaged as leading to management of all resources in such a way that economic, social and aesthetic needs can be fulfilled while maintaining cultural integrity, essential ecological processes, biological diversity and life support systems. Furthermore, Elkington (1997) stated that 'triple bottom line' means expanding the traditional reporting framework to take into account both ecological and social performance to enhance economic performance. All of those three elements should be coherent with each other to ensure quality, continuity and balance between the needs of tourism, protection of the environment and prosperity for the local community, which means that the economic benefit of tourism should be beneficial not only for the companies concerned but also for the local communities as the host. The business entity should be used as a vehicle for coordinating stakeholders' interests, instead of maximising shareholder (owner) profit, so that it can achieve quality, continuity and balance. Good quality, sustainable tourism provides a quality experience for the visitor, while improving the quality of life of the host communities and protecting the quality of the environment. As regards continuity, sustainable tourism ensures the continuity of the natural resources upon which it is based and the continuity of the culture of the host community with satisfying experiences for visitors. Balanced, sustainable tourism balances the needs of the tourism industry, the natural environment and the local communities. Sustainable tourism emphasises mutual goals and cooperation amongst visitors, host communities and destination, in contrast to more traditional approaches to tourism which emphasise their diverse and conflicting needs (UNWTO 2007).

In terms of economic aspect of tourism, development of tourism should give more benefit for local people through community-based tourism approach, which means that tourists, who are willing to have their holiday, must spend their money by staying in the homestay which is located in the village and owned by local people and the food prepared for tourists should be locally produced as most of tourists prefer authenticity of the local products. So, optimising the potential of local agricultural products is crucially needed to be implemented (Suryawardani 2014). Moreover, preserving the environment should also be highlighted. This means, tourists are willing to give more money to be used as the assurance of environmental protection in a destination. Lastly, in terms of social and cultural impacts of tourism development, tourists' activities should not destroy the local culture, but harmony between tourist and local people regarding cultural heritage of destination should also be maintained. Finally, it could be said that benefit of tourism for local people means that tourists are willing to be a part of the system to maintain sustainable tourism in a destination.

2.3 Research Methods

A survey on foreign tourists was undertaken during the period of April to June 2013 in four main destinations in Bali, i.e. Kuta, Nusa Dua, Sanur and Ubud. The locations for this research were selected purposively on the basis that the above destinations are the main tourist destinations in Bali.

The accidental sampling technique (Zikmund 1997) was chosen to select a sample of foreign tourists visiting Bali. The number of foreign tourists who visited Bali in year 2011 was taken to be the population size, which was about 2.6 million. Using the calculation method proposed by Kish (1965: 234) and Yamane (1973) with an error of 5 % (α=0.05), the number of respondents was set at 600. Respondents were interviewed based on a questionnaire.

This study focused mainly on an assessment of the willingness of foreign tourists to participate in the development of Bali's tourism by asking them to what extent they agreed that the money they spent during their visit benefited Balinese people.

Validity and reliability tests were undertaken to examine the truth of data. The validity test is used to examine accuracy and credibility of the results (Sevilla et al. 1993; Simamora 2004; and Zikmund 1997). Product moment correlation (r_{xy}) was calculated (r-value) and compared with the r-table. If the r-value>r-table, this means that the measurement of variables is valid (Sevilla et.al. 1993; Simamora 2004; and Zikmund 1997). In this research, there were 33 questions regarding foreign tourists' perceptions and imported and local products, which were examined through responses from 600 foreign tourists. With the level of significance of 5 %, the critical value was 0.08.

JMP software (SAS Company) version 10 was used in analysing perceptions, preferences and the relationships between variables. JMP is the abbreviation for John's Macintosh Project developed by John Sall and others at SAS Institute in the late 1980s as an interactive statistical visualisation and discovery tool. According to Sall, the JMP name also conveys 'the idea of a lively product that jumped responsively to the user's wishes' (Okerson 2011).

2.4 Survey Results

2.4.1 Opinion, Expectation and Satisfaction of Foreign Tourists

2.4.1.1 Opinion of Accommodation Services

The opinions of foreign tourists regarding the accommodation services were mostly 'very good' (32.50 %), 'extremely good' (32.17 %) and 'good' (27.67 %). Only a few of the respondents were unhappy with the accommodation services, i.e. 'poor' (0.66 %), 'extremely poor' (0.50 %) and 'very poor' (0.33 %). On average, the opinion of foreign visitors on the accommodation services in Bali was 'very good' (5.86 on a 7-point scale). These results show that most of foreign tourists enjoyed the services provided by the accommodations in Bali.

2.4.1.2 Opinion of Restaurant Services

The opinions of foreign tourists regarding restaurant services in Bali were mostly 'very good' (39.00 %), 'good' (36.50 %) and 'extremely good' (15.00 %). Only a few were unhappy with the services of restaurants, i.e. 'poor' (0.67 %), 'very poor' (0.50 %) and 'extremely poor' (0.33 %). On average, the opinion of foreign tourists on restaurant services was 'very good' (5.57 on a 7-point scale). These results show that most of foreign tourists enjoyed the services provided by the restaurants in Bali.

2.4.1.3 Expectation Level Regarding the Whole Trip in Bali

Regarding fulfilment of the expectations of foreign tourists about their whole trips in Bali, most of them said that their expectations matched the reality found in Bali, i.e. 'agreed' (50.17 %), 'extremely agreed' (22.67 %), and 'slightly agreed' (13.33 %). Some of them were still doubtful (9.50 %), but only a few said 'disagreed', namely, 'slightly disagreed' (2.33 %), 'disagreed' (1.50 %) and 'extremely disagreed' (0.50 %). On average, the expectation level was 'agreed' (5.75 on a 7-point scale). These findings show that foreign tourists felt that they got mostly what they expected during their visits in Bali.

2.4.1.4 Emotional Experience

Regarding the emotional experiences of foreign tourists in Bali, most of them said 'pleased' (52.67 %) and 'extremely pleased' (32.67 %). Only a few of them said 'slightly pleased' (7.67 %), 'doubtful' (5.50 %), 'slightly unpleased' (0.67 %), 'unpleased' (0.67 %) or 'extremely unpleased' (0.17 %). On average, the level of emotional experience was 'pleased' (6.09 on a 7-point scale). These results indicate that foreign tourists felt good as they could cool down their emotion during their visits in Bali.

2.4.1.5 Level of Satisfaction with the Whole Trip in Bali

Regarding the levels of satisfaction of foreign tourists with the whole trip in Bali, they mostly said 'satisfied' (53.83 %), 'extremely satisfied' (30.67 %) and 'slightly satisfied' (10.32 %). Only a very few of them said they were unhappy regarding their trips in Bali, namely, 'dissatisfied' (0.67 %), 'extremely dissatisfied' (0.17 %) and 'slightly dissatisfied' (0.17 %). On average, the level of satisfaction was 'satisfied' (6.08 on a 7-point scale). These results indicate that most foreign tourists feel really satisfied with their whole trips in Bali.

2.4.1.6 Level of Agreement on Spending Money to Benefit Balinese People

The results show that 40.50 % of foreign tourists 'agreed', 18.67 % 'slightly agreed' and 16.33 % 'extremely agreed' that their money was spent to benefit Balinese people. On the other hand, some were still 'doubtful' (16.00 %), and a few also 'slightly disagreed' (4.17 %), 'disagreed' (3.50 %) or 'extremely disagreed' (0.83 %). On average, the agreement level on this matter was 'agreed' (5.53 on a 7-point scale). These results indicate that foreign tourists in Bali mostly agreed to spend their money for Balinese people because it could improve the welfare of Balinese people. Furthermore, by improving the quality of life of the host communities, it could lead to the protection of the environmental quality. Therefore, it will provide a better quality of experience for tourists. Towards sustainable tourism, the three elements of triple bottom line should be coherent with each other, in order to improve the quality, continuity and balance between the needs of the tourism industry, protect the environment and enhance the prosperity for the local community. To be able to enhance the prosperity for the local community, the economic benefits from tourism should not only be beneficial for the companies but also for the local communities, as the host (Elkington 1997).

The opinions of foreign tourists on services of accommodation and restaurant, expectation levels concerning the whole trip in Bali, levels of emotional experience, satisfaction levels on the whole trip and levels of agreement regarding spending money for Balinese people are presented in Fig. 2.1.

2.4.2 Analysis of Relationships Between Variables

Analysis of relationships between variables was undertaken to the variables of familiarity (F), satisfaction (S), motivation (M), perceptions on quality of services (P1 and P2), perceptions on quality of imported products and local products (P3 up

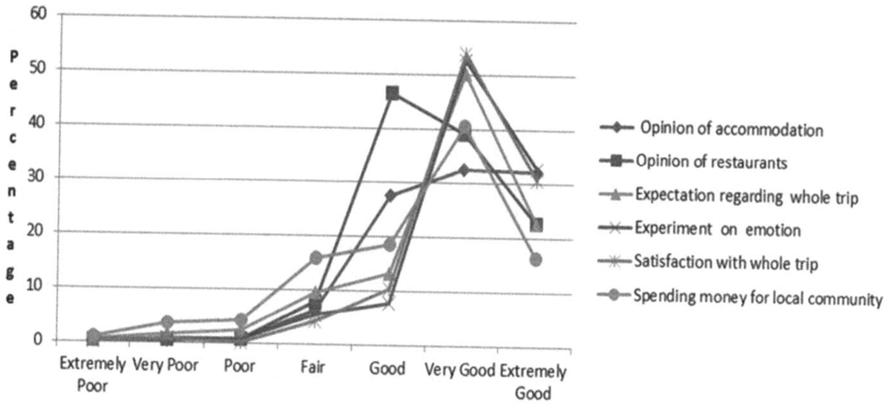

Fig. 2.1 Opinion, expectation and satisfaction of foreign tourists

to P18) and benefit for Balinese people (B). Variables and code of variables of familiarity, satisfaction, motivation, perception and benefits for Balinese can be seen in Table 2.1.

Familiarity is a quality or condition for being familiar which is classified into spatial proximity and expertise of the country (Bashar 2010). Spatial proximity describes proximity to an area, while country expertise is the accumulation of a person's experience of the quality of a destination. In this chapter, familiarity is related to the satisfaction of tourists during their visit in Bali. It was based on 'country of residence' (F1) which covers five continents, namely, Europe, America, Australia, Africa and Asia, while 'large code of residence' (F2) denotes the residential areas where they live, namely, Old Europe, North Europe, East Europe, South Europe, the USA, South America, Africa and Saudi Arabia, Australia, Asia and Indonesia. Meanwhile, country expertise is the accumulation of experience of the quality of a destination (Bashar 2010). In this chapter, it is measured in terms of 'periodicity' in visiting Bali (F3) and 'visit more than 5 times' (F4). All of the above variables influence people's travel choices (Reisinger 2009). This kind of experience was also discussed in this chapter.

2.4.2.1 Relationship Between Familiarity and Satisfaction

Most of variables familiarity (F1, F2 and F4) have significant relationships with variable satisfaction (S), see Fig. 2.2. Variable familiarity F1 (code of country of residence) and F2 (large code of residence) has significant relationships with variables S1 (satisfaction with accommodation and restaurant services in Bali), S2 (satisfaction with the whole trip), S3 (satisfaction level of emotion during visit) and S4 (satisfaction level of expectation). However, variable familiarity F4 (visit more than five times) has a significant relationship only with variable S4 (satisfaction level of expectation).

Table 2.1 Variables and code of variables of familiarity, satisfaction, motivation, perception and benefits for Balinese

No.	Variables	Remarks	Code
1	Familiarity	Country of residence	F1
		Large code of residence	F2
		Periodicity visiting Bali	F3
		Visit more than 5 times	F4
2	Satisfaction	Satisfaction of accommodation and restaurant services in Bali	S1
		Satisfaction of the whole trips	S2
		Satisfaction on the level of emotion during visiting Bali	S3
		Satisfaction on the level of expectation	S4
3	Motivation	Reason for coming (visit friend and relatives/VFR)	M1
		Main purpose	M2
		Activities	M3
4	Perception	Perception on services of:	
		Accommodation	P1
		Restaurants	P2
		Perception of products	
		Imported meat	P3
		Local meat	P4
		Imported fisheries	P5
		Local fisheries	P6
		Imported dairy products	P7
		Local dairy products	P8
		Imported fruits	P9
		Local fruits	P10
		Imported vegetables	P11
		Local vegetables	P12
		Imported beverages	P13
		Local beverages	P14
		Building style	P15
		Furniture	P16
		Room decoration	P17
		Architecture	P18
5	Benefit	Benefits for Balinese	B

Mechanisms in forming interaction between tourists and destinations play an important role in creating a relationship between tourists and destinations. As Lundberg et al. (1991) said that emotional experience of foreign tourists is one of the indicators which can be used to assess the level of satisfaction during visiting a destination. They emphasise that being familiar of a destination is one of the indicators. Their study on customer familiarity and its effects on expectations found that familiarity is significantly associated with performance of perceptions and satisfaction. Their finding is supported by Bashar (2010) who reveals that familiarity influences

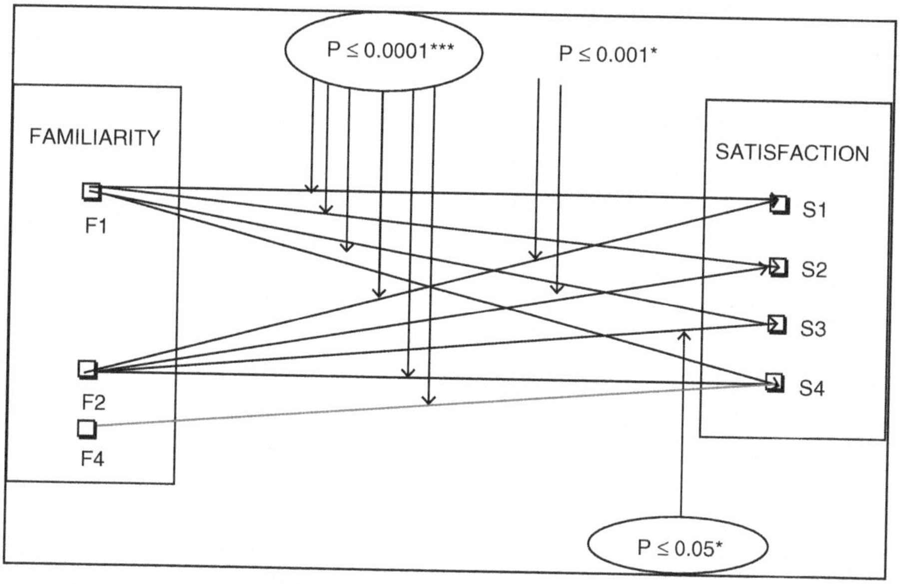

Fig. 2.2 Relationships between familiarity and satisfaction. Remarks: F1 = code of country of residence, F2 = large code of residence, F3 = periodicity of visit, F4 = more than five times visit, S1 = satisfaction with the services of accommodation and restaurant in Bali, S2 = satisfaction with the whole trip, S3 = level of emotion during visit, S4 = level of expectation

satisfaction on travelling which consist of spatial proximity and expertise of the country. Spatial proximity describes proximity to an area, while expertise of the country is the accumulation of a person's experience of the quality of a destination. The results of this study support the above studies that variable familiarity related to spatial proximity, namely, F1 (code of country of residence) and F2 (large code of residence) had significant relationships with variables S1 (satisfaction with accommodation and restaurant services in Bali), S2 (satisfaction with the whole trip), S3 (satisfaction level of emotion during visit) and S4 (satisfaction level of expectation). Variable F1 (code of country of residence) covers five continents, namely, Europe, America, Australia, Africa and Asia, meanwhile variable F2 (large code of residence) denotes the residential areas where they live, namely, Old Europe, North Europe, East Europe, South Europe, the USA, South America, Africa and Saudi Arabia, Australia, Asia and Indonesia. Results of this study indicate that proximity or feeling of closeness to the visiting country influences feeling of being satisfied to a destination.

Another factor of familiarity is accumulation of a person's experience on quality of a destination which consists of F3 (periodicity to visit) and F4 (visit more than 5 times). The periodicity to visit (F3) does not influence tourists' satisfaction. However, visit more than five times (F4) had a significant relationship with variable S4 (satisfaction level of expectation). These results indicate that the more often they visit, the higher the level of satisfaction on their perceived expectation.

2.4.2.2 Relationship Between Familiarity and Perception of Quality of Services and Quality of Products

(a) *Relationship Between Familiarity and Perceptions on Quality of Services (P1 and P2)*

The results show that variable F1 (code of country of residence) had significant relationships with variable P1 (quality of accommodation services) and with variable P2 (quality of restaurant services). In addition, variable F2 (large code of residence) had significant relationships with variable P1 (quality of accommodation services) and with variable P2 (quality of restaurant services), see Fig. 2.3.

(b) *Relationship Between Familiarity and Perceptions on Quality of Products (P3 up to P18)*

There were some significant relationships between variable F (familiarity) and variables P3 up to P18 (perception of the quality of products), as outlined below (see also Fig. 2.4). There were significant relationships between variable F1 (code of country of residence) and the variables of imported meat (P3), local meat (P4), local fishery products (P6), imported dairy products (P7), local fruits (P10), imported beverages (P13), local beverages (P14) and local building style (P15). There were significant relationships between variable F2 (large code of residence) and the variables of imported meat (P3), imported dairy products (P7), imported fruits (P9) and imported vegetables (P11). There were significant relationships between variable F4 (visit more than five times) and the variables of imported meat (P3), imported

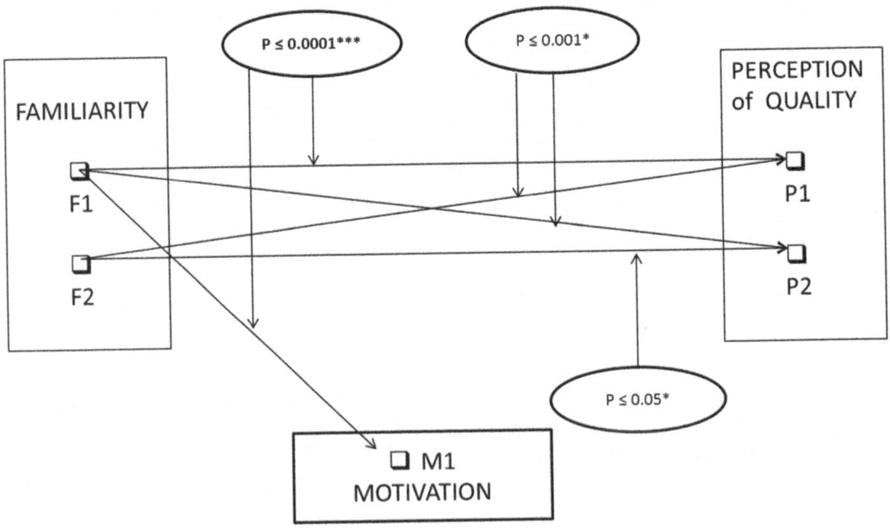

Fig. 2.3 Relationships between familiarity and perceptions on quality, and motivation. Remarks: P1 = quality of accommodation services, P2 = quality of restaurant services, M1 = visit friends and relatives (VFR)

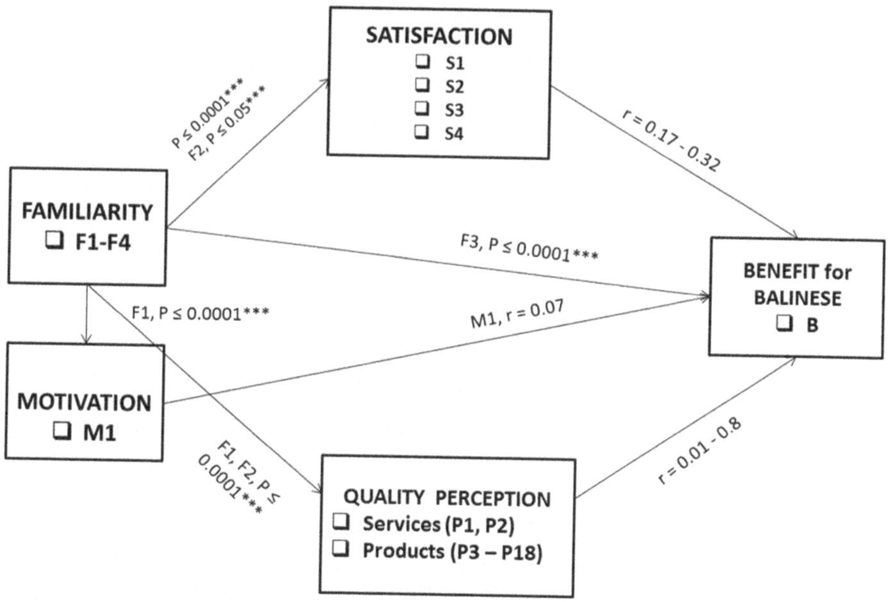

Fig. 2.4 Relationships between variables of familiarity, motivation, satisfaction, perception on quality of services and products and benefit for Balinese

beverages (P13), local beverages (P14) and local building style (P15). However, there was no relationship between variable F3 (periodicity of visit) and perception of the quality of local products. More details can be seen in Table 2.2.

2.4.3 Relationship Between Familiarity and Motivation

Regarding the variables of familiarity (F) and motivation (M), only variable F1 (code of country of residence) had a significant relationship with variable M1 (visit friends and relatives/VFR), see Fig. 2.4. Motivations can be intrinsic (push) or extrinsic (pull). Push motivations correspond to a tourist's desire and emotional frame of mind. Pull motivations represent the attributes of the destination to be visited. Visiting friends and relatives (VFR) was the main reason for coming to Bali, and only variable F1 (code of country of residence) had significant relationship with variable motivation (M). According to Yoon and Uysal (2005), socio-demographic variables are a mediator variable between motivations (either pull or push motivation) and destination loyalty. In case of Bali, desire to do travelling was pushed by the reason on visiting friends and relatives as one of the effects of socio-demographic variables. Being familiar of a destination (Bali) since they have friends and relatives to be visited was the main reason in travelling to Bali. Similar results have been

Table 2.2 Relationship between familiarity and perception on quality of products

Familiarity (F)	Perception on quality of products (P)							
	P3	P4	P5	P6	P7	P8	P9	P10
	Imported Meat	Local meat	Imported fisheries	Local fisheries	Imported dairy products	Local dairy products	Imported fruits	Local fruits
F1	$P \leq 0.05^*$	$P \leq 0.05^*$	ns	$P \leq 0.005^*$	$P \leq 0.05^*$	ns	ns	$P \leq 0.05^*$
F2	$P \leq 0.001^*$	ns	ns	ns	$P \leq 0.001^*$	ns	$P \leq 0.05^*$	ns
F3	ns	ns	ns	ns	ns	ns	ns	ns
F4	$P \leq 0.05^*$	ns	ns	ns	ns	ns	ns	ns

Familiarity (F)	Perception on quality of products (P)							
	P11	P12	P13	P14	P15	P16	P17	P18
	Imported vegetables	Local vegetables	Imported beverages	Local beverages	Local building style	Local furniture	Local room decoration	Local archite cture
F1	ns	ns	$P \leq 0.05^*$	$P \leq 0.001^*$	$P \leq 0.05^*$	ns	ns	ns
F2	$P \leq 0.05^*$	ns	ns	Ns	ns	ns	ns	ns

found in the relationships between familiarity and satisfaction and between familiarity and motivation. These results support the study by Bashar (2010) who reveals that familiarity influences satisfaction on travelling especially on spatial proximity which describes proximity to an area. Proximity or feeling of closeness influences feeling of being motivated to visit friends and relatives to a destination.

2.4.4 Relationship Between Familiarity and Benefit for Balinese

There was a relationship between variable familiarity (F) and the willingness of spending money for Balinese people while visiting Bali (benefit for Balinese, B). The result shows that only variable F3 (periodicity of visits) has a significant relationship with variable B (benefit for Balinese).

2.4.5 Relationship Between Variables Satisfaction and Benefit for Balinese People

Positive correlations were found between all variables of satisfaction (satisfaction with accommodation and restaurant services, with the whole trip, with the level of emotion while visiting Bali and with the level of expectation) and the variable benefit for Balinese people (B). The higher the satisfaction of foreign tourists when visiting Bali, the higher the benefits for Balinese people could be. However, these relationships were relatively weak (coefficient of correlations = 0.17–0.32), see Fig. 2.4.

2.4.6 Relationship Between Variables Motivation and Benefit for Balinese People

A positive correlation was found only between the variable motivation, M1 (visit friends and relatives/VFR) and the variable benefit for Balinese people (B), although the relationship was very weak (coefficient of correlation = 0.07). This result indicates that the more often foreign tourists visiting friends and relatives in Bali, the higher the benefits for Balinese people; see Fig. 2.4.

2.4.7 *Relationship Between Variables Perception Regarding Quality of Services and Products and Variable Benefit for Balinese People*

Positive correlations were found between two variables of perception regarding quality of services (P1 and P2) and the variable benefit for Balinese (B). These correlations ranged from 0.18 to 0.20. Similar results were found between variables of perception regarding the quality of products (P3–P18) and the variable benefit for Balinese people (B). The correlations between all variables of perceptions regarding the quality of local products and the variable benefit for Balinese ranged from 0.01 to 0.80. Several variables of perception regarding the quality of local products had relatively strong correlations with the variable benefit for Balinese people (B), namely, local furniture, P16 ($r=0.8$); local vegetables, P12 ($r=0.7$); and local building style, P15 ($r=0.5$). These mean that the higher the perception of quality of local products and services, the higher the benefits for Balinese people; see Fig. 2.4.

There were also some significant relationships between variable familiarity (F) and the variables of perception of quality of services and products (P1–P18). The positive correlations were also found between perceptions regarding the quality of services and local products and the benefit for Balinese people ($r=0.01$–0.8). Several perceptions of the quality of local products had relatively strong correlations with the benefit for Balinese, namely, local furniture ($r=0.8$), local vegetables ($r=0.7$) and local building style ($r=0.5$). These mean that the higher the perception of the quality of local products and services, the higher the benefits for Balinese people. This finding supports the study by Goodrich (1978), Solomon (1999) and Andriotis (2005) who found that tourist behaviour in choosing a destination has a significant relationship to the perception of tourists on a destination.

2.5 Future and Emerging Trends

Improvement the quality of products and services of tourism industry in Bali is crucial to be undertaken in order to improve the level of satisfaction of foreign tourists in visiting Bali. This could lead to an increase of the willingness of foreign tourists to spend money for local Balinese. The role of stakeholders of Bali tourism is very important through integrated coordination in all aspects of tourism development, so that development of tourism brings about improvement of the quality of life of the Balinese. Community empowerment should become the basis of tourism development in Bali; therefore, tourism in Bali will bring maximum benefits for local community.

2.6 Conclusion

The opinion of foreign tourists regarding the services provided by the accommodations and restaurants in Bali was 'very good' (5.86 and 5.57 on a 7-point scale, respectively,). These results show that most of foreign tourists enjoyed the services provided by the accommodations and restaurants in Bali. Regarding the fulfilment of the expectation of foreign tourists about the whole trip in Bali, the level of agreement was 'agreed' (5.75 on a 7-point scale). This finding shows that foreign tourists felt that they got mostly what they expected during their visit in Bali. The level of emotional experience of foreign tourists in Bali was 'pleased' (6.09 on a 7-point scale). This result indicates that foreign tourists felt good as they could cool down their emotion during their visits in Bali. The level of satisfaction with the whole trip in Bali was 'satisfied' (6.08 on a 7-point scale). The results indicate that most of foreign tourists felt really satisfied with their whole trips in Bali. Level of agreement on their spending money to benefit Balinese people was 'agreed' (5.53 on a 7-point scale). The results indicate that foreign tourists in Bali mostly agree to spend their money for Balinese people because it could improve the welfare of Balinese people.

Regarding relationships between variables motivation, satisfaction, perception of quality of services and benefit for Balinese people, the results show that most of variables familiarity (F) had significant relationships with all of variables satisfaction (S), and only variable F3 (periodicity of visits) had a significant relationship with the variable B (benefit for Balinese). There were also some significant relationships between variable familiarity (F) and the variables of perception of quality of services and products (P1–P18). The positive correlations were also found between perceptions regarding the quality of services and local products and the benefit for Balinese people ($r=0.01$–0.8). Several perceptions of the quality of local products had relatively strong correlations with the benefit for Balinese, namely, local furniture ($r=0.8$), local vegetables ($r=0.7$) and local building style ($r=0.5$). These results indicate that the higher the perception of the quality of local products and services, the higher the benefits for Balinese people could be.

Based on the statistical results, it can be concluded that most of the tourists who visit Bali are willing to spend their money to the local people and to be a part of the system of Bali tourism in terms of maintaining sustainable tourism in Bali. Most of the tourists are also willing to spend their money and would love to stay in the village and prefer authenticity of the local products. Most of foreign tourists also prefer staying in the locally decorated Balinese style accommodation and are willing to spend more money for environmental protection in order to minimise negative impacts of tourism development in Bali, as long as the mechanism for this is well organised by government and the people of Bali. They would also love to live a harmonious interaction with local Balinese people and are willing to maintain cultural heritage of Bali as one of the famous attractive destination in the world. Their opinion, expectation and expression of satisfaction of the whole trip to Bali show that they found what they expected during their visit to Bali, and there is no doubt they will be responsible for the long-term development of tourism in Bali.

References

Alexandros A, Shabbar J (2005) Stated preferences for two Cretan heritage attractions. Ann Tour Res 32(4):985–1005

Allesi SM, Trollip SR (1991) Computer-based instruction: methods and development. Prentice-Hall, Inc., Upper Saddle River

Andriotis K (2005) Community groups' perceptions of and preferences for tourism development: evidence from Crete. J Hosp Tour Res 29:67–89

Baker DA, Crompton JL (2000) Quality, satisfaction and behavioural intentions. Ann Tour Res 27(3):785–804

Bashar A (2010) An analysis of push and pull travel motivations of foreign tourists to Jordan. Int J Busi Manag 5(12):41–50

Bauer H, Mark G, Leach M (2002) Building customer relations over the internet. Ind Mark Manag 31(2):155–163

Beerli A, Martín JD (2004) Tourists' characteristics and the perceived image of tourist destinations: a quantitative analysis – a case study of Lanzarote, Spain. Tour Manag 25(5):623–636

Bigné JE, Sánchez MI, Sánchez J (2001) Tourism image, evaluation variables and after purchase behaviour: inter-relationship. Tour Manag 22(6):607–616

Bigné JE, Andreu L, Gnoth J (2005) The theme park experience: an analysis of pleasure, arousal and satisfaction. Tour Manag 26(6):833–844

Bitner MJ (1990) Evaluating service encounter: the effects of physical surroundings and employee responses. J Mark 54:69–82

Bowen D (2001) Antecedents of consumer satisfaction and dis-satisfaction (CS/D) on long-haul inclusive tours: a reality check on theoretical considerations. Tour Manag 22(1):49–61

Bramwell B (1998) User satisfaction and product development in urban tourism. Tour Manag 19(1):35–47

Brodie RJ, Coviello NE, Brookes RW, Victoria L (1997) Towards a paradigm shift in marketing: an examination of current marketing practices. J Mark Manag 13(5):383–406

Cai LA, Wu B, Bai B (2003) Destination image and loyalty. Cognizant Commun Corp 7:153–162

Chen J, Gursoy D (2001) An investigation of tourists' destination loyalty and preferences. Int J Contemp Hosp Manag 13(2):79–85

Court B, Lupton R (1997) Customer portfolio development: modelling destination adopters, inactives, and rejecters. J Travel Res 36(1):35–43

Davis, C.H. 2003. Traveler perceptions of a destination as a source of new product concepts: Q-Method study of summer visitors to the bay of Fundy. Paper presented on TTRA Canada Annual Conference, Saint John, New Brunswick, October. http://www.ryerson.ca/~c5davis/publications/Davis%20-%20traveler%20perceptions%20as%20source%20of%20new%20product%20concepts.pdf. Accessed Jan. 6, 2015.

Dick AS, Basu K (1994) Customer loyalty: toward an integrated conceptual framework. J Acad Mark Sci 22(2):99–113

Elkington J (1997) Cannibals with forks: the triple bottom line (TBL) of 21st century business. Capstone, Oxford

Flavian C, Martinez E, Polo Y (2001) Loyalty to grocery stores in the Spanish market of the 1990s. J Retail Consum Serv 8:85–93

Font AR (2000) Mass tourism and the demand for protected natural areas: a travel cost approach. J Environ Econ Manag 39(1):97–116

Fornell C (1992) A national customer satisfaction barometer: the Swedish experience. J Mark 56(1):6–21

Goodrich JN (1978) The relationship between preferences for and perceptions of vacation destinations: application of a choice model. J Travel Res 17:8–13

Hallowell R (1996) The relationship of customer satisfaction, customer loyalty, and profitability: an empirical study. Int J Serv Ind Manag 7(4):27–42

Higgins ET, Freitas LC, Spiegel AL, Molden DC (2003) Transfer of value from fit. J Pers Soc Psychol 84(6):1140–1153
Homburg C, Giering A (2001) Personal characteristics as moderators of the relationship between customer satisfaction and loyalty – an empirical analysis. Psychol Mark 18(1):43–66
Khan MS (1991) Methods of motivating to increase productivity. J Manag Eng 12(2):25–31
Kim H, Jamal T (2007) Touristic quest for existential authenticity. Ann Tour Res 34(1):181–201
Kish L (1965) Survey sampling. Wiley, New York
Kotler PR (1993) Marketing management: analysis, planning, implementation and control. Prentice-Hall, Englewood Cliffs
Kozak M, Rimmington M (2000) Tourism satisfaction with Mallorca, Spain, as an off-season holiday destination. J Travel Res 38(3):260–269
La Barbara PA, Mazursky D (1983) A longitudinal assessment of consumer satisfaction/dissatisfaction: the dynamic aspect of the cognitive process. J Mark Res 20:393–404
Lin S, Li C, You C (2012) Consumer behavior and perception of marketing strategy for amusement parks: a case study of Taiwan. Afr J Busi Manag 6(14):4795–4803
Lundberg D, Krishnamoorthy EM, Stavenga MH (1991) Tourism economics. Wiley, New York
Lunenborg FC (2011) Expectancy theory of motivation: motivating by altering expectations. Int J Manag Busi Admin 15(1):1–6
Mazursky D (1989) Past experience and future tourism decisions. Ann Tour Res 16:333–344
Mill RC, Morrison AM (2009) The tourism system. Kendall Hunt Publishing Company, Dubuque
Mittal V, Kamakura WA (2001) Satisfaction, repurchase intent and repurchase behavior: investigating the moderating effect of customer characteristics. J Mark Res 38(1):131–142
Niininen O, Szivas E, Riley M (2004) Destination loyalty and repeat behaviour: an application of optimum stimulation measurement. Int J Tour Res 6(6):439–447
Noe FP, Uysal M (1997) Evaluation of outdoor recreational settings: a problem of measuring user satisfaction. J Retail Consum Serv 4(4):223–230
Oh H (1999) Service quality, customer satisfaction, and customer value: a holistic perspective. Int J Hospit Manag 18:67–82
Okerson BB (2011) Paper JP-03 JMP in: a SAS programmer's look at JMP Barbara B. Okerson WellPoint, Richmond, VA. (cited 9 December 2013). Available from URL: http://analytics.ncsu.edu/sesug/2011/JP03.Okerson.pdf
Oppermann M (2000) Tourism destination loyalty. J Travel Res 39(1):78–84
Oliver RL (1999) Whence consumer loyalty? J Mark 63(special issue):33–44
Petrick JF (2004) Are loyal visitors desired visitors? Tour Manage 25(4):463–470
Petrick JF, Morais D, Norman W (2001) An examination of the determinants of entertainment vacationers' intention to revisit. J Travel Res 40(1):41–48
Pinder CC (1987) Valence-instrumentality-expectancy theory. In: Steers RM, Porter LW (eds) Motivation and work behavior. McGraw-Hill, New York, pp 69–89
Pine BJ, Peppers D, Rogers M (1995) Do you want to keep your customers forever? Harv Bus Rev 73:103–114
Reisinger Y (2009) International tourism: cultures and behavior. Elsevier, Oxford
Ross RL, Iso-Ahola SE (1991) Sightseeing tourists' motivation and satisfaction. Ann Tour Res 18(2):226–237
Schofield PS (2000) Evaluating Castlefield urban heritage park from the consumer perspective: destination attribute importance, visitor perception, and satisfaction. Tour Anal 5(2–4):183–189
Sevilla CG, Ochava JA, Punsalam TG, Regala BP, Uriarte GG (1993) Research method. University of Indonesia, Jakarta
Simamora B (2004) Panduan riset perilaku konsumen. PT. Gramedia Pustaka Utama, Jakarta
Solomon M (1999) Consumer behaviour: buying, having and being. Prentice-Hall, Inc., Upper Saddle River
Suryawardani IGAO (2014) Tourism leakage from the accommodation in Bali. Unpublished PhD dissertation. Udayana University, Denpasar
Swarbrooke J, Horner S (2009) Consumer behaviour in tourism, 2nd edn. Elsevier, Oxford

Turnbull P, Wilson DT (1989) Developing and protecting profitable customer relationships. Ind Mark Manag 18:233–238

Um S, Chon K, Ro Y (2006) Antecedents of revisit intention. Ann Tour Res 33(4):1141–1158

UNWTO (2007) A practical guide to tourism destination management. United Nation World Tourism Organisation, Madrid

Waite M, Hawker S (eds) (2009) Oxford paperback dictionary & thesaurus. Oxford University Press, Oxford

Weaver PA, McCleary KW, Lepisto L, Damonte LT (1994) The relationship of destination selection attributes to psychological, behavioural and demographic variables. J Hospital Leis Market 2(2):93–109

Woodside A, Lysonski S (1989) A general model of traveller destination choice. J Travel Res 27(4):8–14

Yamane (1973) Determining sample size. Chapter 3. Methodology. [cited 2012 Jun. 6]. Available from URL: www.thapra.lib.su.acth/objects/thesis/fulltex/thapra/…/chapter3.pdf

Yoon Y, Uysal M (2005) An examination of the effects of motivation and satisfaction on destination loyalty: a structural model. Tour Manag 26(1):45–56

Zikmund GW (1997) Business research methods. The Dryden Press, Fort Worth

Zimmer Z, Brayley RE, Searle MS (1995) Whether to go and where to go: identification of important influences on seniors' decisions to travel. J Travel Res 33(3):3–10

I Gusti Ayu Oka Suryawardani Field of Study: Tourism Economic and Sustainable Tourism Development.

Agung Suryawan Wiranatha Field of Study: Tourism Planning and Sustainable Tourism Development.

Christine Petr Professor in Marketing EIREST, Sorbonne Universitė Paris1, Paris, France

Chapter 3
Destination Loyalty Model of Senior Foreign Tourists Visiting Bali Tourism Destination

I. Gusti Bagus Rai Utama

Abstract In the recent years, the senior foreign tourist segment has become increasingly important for the tourism industry. The strength of this market segment lies in its two characteristics: the purchasing power and the time available for travel. This research was conducted based on these two considerations. This research is confirmatory to the loyalty model developed by previous research, but specifically studied foreign senior tourists. The 400 respondents for this research were determined purposively. The criteria were senior tourists aged 55 or over and tourists vacationing in one of Bali's tourism destinations. Descriptive statistical analysis and the SEM-AMOS structural model analysis tools were utilized. Meanwhile, the qualitative analysis is descriptive to complement the quantitative analysis. The demographic profiles of the respondents composed of 57 % male travelers and 43 % female. Tourists in the age group of 55–65 are 73 and 27 % over 65 years. Repeat visitors are 81 and 19 % first time visitors. The findings of this research indicated that (1) internal motivation does not have a significant effect on destination image, (2) external motivation has a significant effect on destination image and loyalty, but does not have a significant effect on tourist's satisfaction, (3) destination image has a significant effect on tourist's satisfaction, and (4) tourist's satisfaction has a significant effect on destination loyalty. Two loyalty models were formed: (1) Destination loyalty is directly influenced by tourist's satisfaction and indirectly influenced by destination image and external motivation. (2) Destination loyalty is directly influenced by external motivation, but the influence is not as significant as the influence of tourist's satisfaction on loyalty. Theoretically, the research suggests maintaining the joint approach because this approach is able to answer various questions that quantitative approach alone cannot answer completely. From a practical perspective, the preservation of Bali's destination image was found to be adequate. The image of Bali includes: (1) a destination that has cultural uniqueness, (2) welcoming local inhabitants, (3) comprehensive tourism infrastructure, and (4) comfortable tourism atmosphere.

I.G.B.R. Utama (✉)
Universitas Dhyana Pura, Bali, Indonesia
e-mail: raiutama@undhirabali.ac.id

P. Mandal, J. Vong (eds.), *Development of Tourism and the Hospitality Industry in Southeast Asia*, Managing the Asian Century,
DOI 10.1007/978-981-287-606-5_3

Keywords Senior foreign tourists • Internal motivation • External motivation • Destination image • Tourist's satisfaction • Tourist's loyalty

3.1 Introduction

The phenomenon that prompted this study is the rapid growth of the senior population segment around the world. A person who has reached the age of 55 and above is considered senior. The continuous growth of this age group has created a new market segment for the tourism industry. Two distinct profile characteristics considered attractive for the tourism industry are the high purchasing power and availability of leisure time because generally seniors have retired or are retiring. However, it should be noted that the senior groups also have different motivation from other age groups, demanding more and better healthcare facilities and travel assistance especially for those in the 75–80 and the 80 and above age groups. In order for Bali to capture this market opportunity of senior travelers, a survey on senior tourists visiting Bali is deemed necessary. The lack of a theoretical study on motivation, destination image, tourist's satisfaction, and destination loyalty of senior foreign tourists is also the reason the study was conducted, because the factors affecting the loyalty of senior foreign tourists on Bali as a destination have yet to be explained in depth.

Based on the abovementioned problems, the main subject matter in the current study is how do motivation, destination image, and tourist's satisfaction affect the loyalty of senior foreign tourists visiting Bali, with the sub-questions as follows:

1. How does internal motivation of senior foreign tourists affect the destination image of Bali?
2. How does external motivation of senior foreign tourists affect the destination image of Bali?
3. How does internal motivation affect the satisfaction of senior foreign tourists visiting Bali?
4. How does external motivation affect the satisfaction of senior foreign tourists visiting Bali?
5. How does internal motivation of affect the destination loyalty of senior foreign tourists visiting Bali?
6. How does external motivation of affect the destination loyalty of senior foreign tourists visiting Bali?
7. How does the destination image of Bali affect the satisfaction of senior foreign tourists visiting Bali?
8. How does tourist's satisfaction affect destination loyalty of senior foreign tourists visiting Bali?
9. What are the direct, indirect, and the combined effects of internal motivation, external motivation, destination image of Bali, and tourist's satisfaction on the destination loyalty of senior foreign tourists visiting Bali?
10. What is the destination loyalty model of senior foreign tourists visiting Bali?

Based on the issues formulated, the general purpose of the present study is:

The general objective of this study is to analyze and determine the effects of motivation, destination image, and tourist's satisfaction on the loyalty of senior foreign tourists visiting Bali. The specific objectives of the research are aimed at addressing some of the sub-issues that have been determined, which are as follows:

1. To analyze and determine the effects of internal motivation of senior foreign tourists on the destination image of Bali.
2. To analyze and determine the effects of external motivation of senior foreign tourists on the destination image of Bali.
3. To analyze and determine the effects of internal motivation on the satisfaction of senior foreign tourists visiting Bali.
4. To analyze and determine the effects of external motivation on the satisfaction of senior foreign tourists visiting Bali.
5. To analyze and determine the effects of internal motivation on the destination loyalty of senior foreign tourists visiting Bali.
6. To analyze and determine the effects of external motivation on the destination loyalty of senior foreign tourists visiting Bali.
7. To analyze and determine the effects of Bali's destination image on the satisfaction of senior foreign tourists visiting Bali.
8. To analyze and determine the effects of tourist's satisfaction on the destination loyalty of senior foreign tourists visiting Bali.
9. To analyze and determine direct, indirect, and the combined effects of internal motivation, external motivation, destination image of Bali, and tourist's satisfaction on the destination loyalty of senior foreign tourists visiting Bali.
10. To test and determine the feasibility of the loyalty model of senior foreign tourists visiting Bali.

This research is directed to contribute theoretically and practically on the marketing of tourism destinations, especially in relation to motivation, destination image, tourist's satisfaction, and destination loyalty of senior foreign tourists traveling to a tourism destination. The theoretical significance of this research for the development of tourism science is to test the hypotheses and to test the validity of the models developed by Yoon and Uysal (2003) and Chi (2005) and combining the two models to determine a loyalty model specifically for senior foreign tourists. The formation of destination loyalty model for senior foreign tourists incorporating travel motivation, destination image, and tourist's satisfaction is expected to be further confirmed by subsequent researchers to establish the loyalty model for senior in tourists on Bali as a tourism destination. On a practical level, the loyalty of senior foreign tourists can be used as a model in determining loyalty if a destination seeks to reach the senior market segment. The identification of travel motivation for senior tourists visiting Bali is hoped to contribute in determining supply and demand dimensions for Bali's tourism products. The identification of tourist's satisfaction is hoped to contribute in determining destination quality, in order to determine senior tourists' loyalty. Another significance of this research is as a consideration when determining tourism target market, specifically for the senior segment in relation to: (1) devising a more effective promotional strategies, (2) the provision of products and services more closely aligned with the expectations of senior tourists, (3) determining distribution channels, and (4) determining more competitive pricing so that tourists prefer to travel to Bali than other destinations in Asia.

3.2 Literature Review

3.2.1 Senior Tourists

The definition of "senior" is still widely debated, particularly with regard to the age at which a person is called senior. According to Patterson (2006: 17) "older people" refers to people from the age of 55 and beyond. Likewise, the definition of the World Tourism Organization (2005) explains that senior travelers are senior tourists aged 55 years or more. The Indonesian government also defines it such as that senior foreign tourists are senior travelers who are foreign nationals who are at least 55 years of age. This definition is adopted from the Presidential Decree number 31 of 1998. In this study, the definition of senior foreign tourist refers to the chronological age of 55 years and beyond.

3.2.2 Travel Motivation

Travel motivation is divided into two types of motivation: internal and external. Pitana and Gayatri (2005) considered internal motivation as the push factor for people to travel, which means that they are driven by certain motives to travel. Further, it was said that motivation is a basic foundation in the study of tourists and tourism, because motivation is the driving factor for the process of traveling. Travel motivation is also considered part of psychological needs and wants, as well as biological ones, which include inseparable push and pull factors that drive people to do or conduct tourism activities (Uysal and Hagan 1993; Iso-Ahola 1991; Yoon and Uysal 2003).

3.2.3 Destination Image

Milman and Pizam (1995) cognitively offered three components that make up the image of a tourism destination, namely, attraction, attitudes, and behavior of the hosts, and the destination environment such as climate, facilities, and so on. Meanwhile, Ritchie et al. (1993) identified that cognitively, destination image comprises of psychological components, uniqueness, and destination attributes, which holistically make up the image of a destination. Further, Beerli and Martin (2004) (in Chi 2005) studied and classified nine attributes that affect the image of a destination, namely: (1) natural attributes, (2) opportunities for leisure and recreation, (3) natural environment, (4) public facilities, (5) culture, history, and art, (6) social environment, (7) tourism infrastructure, (8) economic and political conditions, and (9) atmosphere of the destination.

3.2.4 Tourist's Satisfaction

According to Kotler (2003: 61), customer satisfaction is a function of customer expectation on the service received. Customers attain satisfaction from the services provided by a company if the service meets the expectation of quality and is in accordance with the customer's expectation. Consumer satisfaction is one indicator that affects loyalty. The higher the level of satisfaction, and the higher the level of loyalty, accordingly Zeithaml and Bitner (2000: 287) stated that customer satisfaction is the fulfillment of consumer response. Oliver (1999: 392) argued that customer satisfaction is the evaluation of the surprise inherent in the acquisition of a product or experience. Simply put, satisfied customers are great assets for a company's survival. Maintaining customer satisfaction should be done as a management of quality for the services offered so that customer satisfaction can be maintained.

3.2.5 Destination Loyalty

In the field of marketing, repeat purchases and willingness to recommend to potential buyers are good indicators of customer loyalty. The degree of consumer loyalty is one of the indicators used to measure the success of a marketing strategy (Flavian et al. 2001). The same is true in the field of tourism marketing. As a product tourists may come back (revisit) or recommend a destination to friends, family, and others as potential tourists. In this context, the study of consumer loyalty is applicable in the field of tourism, in which tourism is a product or service marketed tourists in the increasingly competitive destination marketing competition (Dimanche and Havitz 1994). Contextualization of tourist's loyalty to a travel destination refers to the consistency of certain tourists in visiting a specific destination even though other competing destinations offer newer attractions with superior attributes or quality. In the tourism industry, there is empirical evidence indicating that satisfaction is a strong indicator of loyalty for tourists to come back again and again to a destination, and those loyal tourists are good marketers for the destination as they tend to share stories and recommendations to friends, family, relatives, and others to visit the destination they have visited (Chi 2005).

3.3 Conceptual Framework and Research Hypotheses

3.3.1 Conceptual Framework

There are five latent variables in this study, consisting of internal motivation (exogenous), external motivation (exogenous), destination image (endogenous), satisfaction (endogenous), and loyalty (endogenous). Latent variables are nonmeasurable variables, so it is necessary to measure certain indicators in accordance to existing theories (Ferdinand 2002: 59). The underlying concept in this study is the concept of tourist loyalty. This concept of loyalty has been built by previous studies (Yoon and Uysal 2003; Chi 2005). The loyalty model constructed by Yoon and Uysal (2003) illustrated that loyalty is formed by tourist motivation mediated by satisfaction variable, while the loyalty model constructed by Chi (2005) illustrated that loyalty is formed by destination image mediated by destination attributes and overall satisfaction.

From the two models, this researcher attempts to combine the previous models that have been confirmed by Yoon and Uysal (2003) and Chi (2005) to form a new model illustrating that destination loyalty is formed by internal and external motivation through the variables of destination image and satisfaction of senior foreign tourists. Furthermore, the operationalization variable of loyalty is translated into two indicators: willingness to recommend and the desire for repeat visits (Yoon and Uysal 2003; dan Chi 2005).

The theoretical framework is shown in Fig. 3.1.

3.3.2 Research Hypotheses

Based on the above concept, eight research hypotheses are proposed as follows:

1. Internal motivation of senior foreign tourists affects the destination image of Bali.
2. External motivation of senior foreign tourists affects the destination image of Bali.
3. Internal motivation affects the satisfaction of senior foreign tourists visiting Bali.
4. External motivation affects the satisfaction of senior foreign tourists visiting Bali.
5. Internal motivation affects the destination loyalty of senior foreign tourists visiting Bali.
6. External motivation affects the destination loyalty of senior foreign tourists visiting Bali.
7. The destination image of Bali affects the satisfaction of senior foreign tourists visiting Bali.
8. Tourist's satisfaction affects destination loyalty of senior foreign tourists visiting Bali.

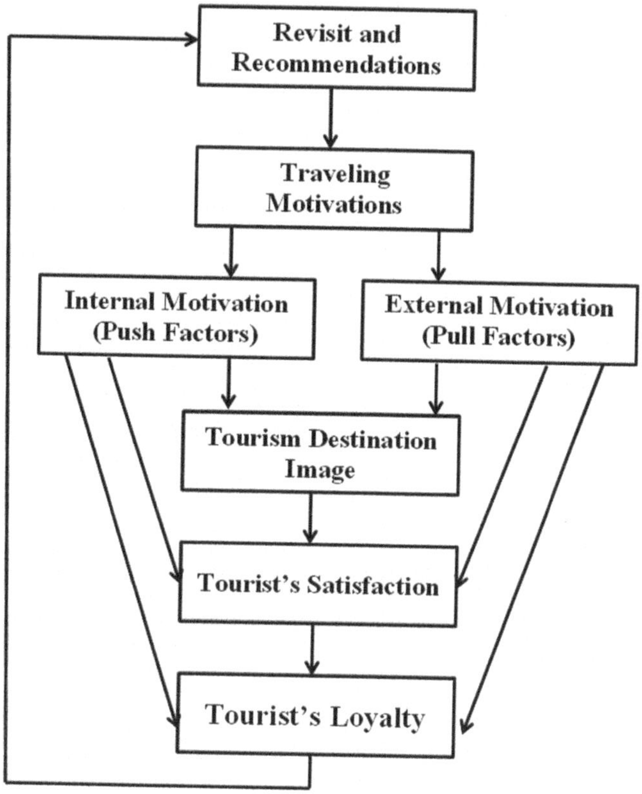

Fig. 3.1 Theoretical framework (Source: Yoon and Uysal 2003; Chi 2005)

3.4 Research Methods

This study is a confirmatory to the loyalty model developed by Yoon and Uysal (2003) and Chi (2005), with a distinct focus on senior foreign tourists. The research involved 400 purposively determined respondents, which referred to foreign nationals aged 55 years and above who were visiting one of five tourism areas in Bali, namely, Kuta, Nusa Dua, Sanur, Ubud, and Lovina. Quantitative and qualitative analysis tools are used to process the data. The quantitative data analysis tools utilized in this study are descriptive statistical analysis and the SEM-AMOS structural model analysis. Meanwhile, the quantitative analysis tool utilized is descriptive qualitative analysis that aims to clarify and complement the quantitative analysis. The research variables and indicators consist of (Table 3.1):

Table 3.1 Definitions of variables and indicators

Variable	Code	Indicator
X1 internal motivation	$X_{1.1}$	Rest and relaxation
	$X_{1.2}$	Visiting new places
	$X_{1.3}$	Knowledge and experiences
	$X_{1.4}$	Escaping the routine
	$X_{1.5}$	Meeting new people and socializing
	$X_{1.6}$	Health and fitness
	$X_{1.7}$	Physical exercise
	$X_{1.8}$	Visiting friends and family
X2 external motivation	$X_{2.1}$	History of Bali
	$X_{2.2}$	Culture of Bali
	$X_{2.3}$	Nature of Bali
	$X_{2.4}$	Prices in Bali
	$X_{2.5}$	Events and festival
	$X_{2.6}$	Holiday or leisure
	$X_{2.7}$	Transportation
	$X_{2.8}$	Distance from home country
	$X_{2.9}$	Food and beverage
	$X_{2.10}$	Facilities and service
	$X_{2.11}$	Healthcare facilities
	$X_{2.12}$	Immigration procedure and service
	$X_{2.13}$	Security
	$X_{2.14}$	Service from travel agencies
	$X_{2.15}$	Tour leaders and guides
Destination image	$Y_{1.1}$	Tourism activities
	$Y_{1.2}$	Natural beauty
	$Y_{1.3}$	Culture of Bali
	$Y_{1.4}$	People of Bali
	$Y_{1.5}$	Tourism infrastructure
	$Y_{1.6}$	Political and economic stability
	$Y_{1.7}$	Atmosphere of Bali
Tourist's satisfaction	$Y_{2.1}$	Attraction
	$Y_{2.2}$	Accessibility
	$Y_{2.3}$	Tourism facilities
	$Y_{2.4}$	Service
Loyalty	$Y_{3.1}$	Repeat visit
	$Y_{3.2}$	Willingness to recommend

Sources: Yoon and Uysal (2003), Chi (2005), Esichaikul (2012)

3.5 Findings and Analysis

3.5.1 Description of Research Data

The number of respondents was 400, with 57 % male respondents and 43 % female, 73 % aged between 55 and 65 years and 27 % 65 years over, 41 % came from Australia and 59 came form others, and 81 % of respondents were repeat visitors and 19 % first visitors. Strong motives that push senior foreign tourists to travel are the need for rest and relaxation, visiting new places, seeking new knowledge and experience, getting out of the routine, meeting new people, and socializing. Meanwhile, improving health and fitness, physical exercise, and visiting family and friends are not strong push motivation to encourage senior foreign tourists to travel.

Strong pull factors that motivate senior foreign tourists to travel to Bali are the interests in Balinese culture, natural beauty of Bali, the history of Bali, gains on holiday in Bali, Bali's diverse culinary, and the prices of goods/services in Bali. Meanwhile, security, development of transportation, healthcare facilities, the quality of tour leaders and guides, the service of travel agencies, and the immigration procedures are not strong pull motivational factors that appeal senior foreign tourists in choosing Bali as a destination.

Until now, Bali as a tourism destination still has a good image, such as Bali is positioned as a tourism destination with culture, history, and art. Bali also has a positioning image as a good travel destination for vacation and recreation. Another image of Bali is that the island has a good social environment and a complete tourism infrastructure. However, certain image of Bali is on the decline, including the natural environment of Bali which is considered to be increasingly more, atmosphere of Bali which is considered to be increasingly crowded, as well as the political and economic stability of Bali which is considered to be less supportive.

Related to satisfaction of senior tourists, some attributes are considered adequate and in accordance to the expectations of senior foreign tourists visiting Bali. These attributes include tourism infrastructure, tourist attractions, travel experience to and within Bali, tourist services throughout Bali, and the availability of various tourism facilities.

3.5.2 Results of Hypotheses Testing and Research Findings

The findings of this study are in contrast to the findings of Yoon and Uysal (2003) and Chi (2005), although there is similar relationship between the variables in each model. Figure 3.2 is the final model after considering several criteria for the model's goodness of fit.

This study is able to address eight research questions, which can be explained as follows: (1) Internal motivation does not have a significant effect on destination

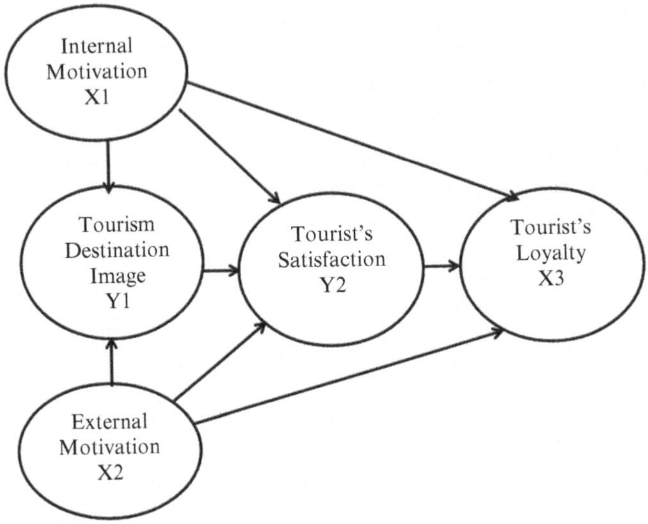

Fig. 3.2 Relationships between research variables (Note: The value of direct effects is based on standardized regression weights, and the dotted arrows signify less significant relationships)

image, which means that in order to create a good destination image, internal travel motivation alone is insufficient, but external motivation should create a wholesome appeal motivation factor to visit a destination. (2) External motivation of senior foreign tourists has a significant effect the destination image of Bali. Strong pull indicators include is the appeal of culture, nature, history of Bali, the benefits of vacationing in Bali, Bali's culinary diversity, and the prices of goods/services. (3) Internal motivation of senior foreign tourists does not have a significant effect on tourist This finding suggests that satisfying factors in the forms of tourism attributes in Bali is not sufficient to satisfy the pull motivational factors for the senior traveler respondents. (4) External motivation also does not have a significant effect on the satisfaction of senior foreign tourists visiting Bali.

This indicates that Bali's tourism attributes of destination are not yet in line with expectations (satisfaction) of senior foreign tourists visiting Bali. (5)Internal motivation of senior foreign tourists does not have a significant effect on loyalty because that finding is not supported by empirical data.

The direction of the relationship between internal motivation and tourist loyalty is negative, which signifies a negative relationship, or the higher the push factor, the lower the level of loyalty for Bali as one specific destination. (6) External motivation factors (destination attributes) have a significant effect on tourist loyalty. (7) Destination image has a significant effect on the satisfaction of the senior foreign tourists visiting Bali. The image of Bali as a tourism destination including indicators such as the uniqueness of Balinese culture, friendly people, tourism infrastructure, facilities, and a comfortable atmosphere was perceived positively by the senior foreign respondents. (8) The satisfaction of senior foreign tourists has a significant effect on destination loyalty.

Fig. 3.3 Loyalty model of senior foreign tourists visiting Bali (Source: Yoon and Uysal 2003; Chi 2005; Esichaikul 2012)

The findings of this study are a model of senior foreign tourists' loyalty consisting of two paths. Graphically, the findings on the loyalty model of senior foreign tourists visiting Bali can be represented as follows (Fig. 3.3).

In the first path, seen from the value of the standardized regression weights coefficients, destination image variable has the most significant effect on tourist satisfaction. Then, the external motivation variable has a significant influence on destination image, and tourist satisfaction variable has a significant effect on destination loyalty. On the contrary, in the second path, from the values of standardized regression weights coefficients, external motivation variables have a direct effect on destination loyalty, but the effect is not as strong as the destination image variable and tourist satisfaction. External motivation variable has direct and indirect effects on destination loyalty, so it can be concluded that external motivation is a variable that has an important role in forming destination loyalty.

3.6 Conclusion and Recommendations

3.6.1 Conclusion

The loyalty model for senior foreign tourists is associated with various dynamic variables and indicators in line with the dynamism of a tourism destination, so periodic research is advisable by continually carefully testing theoretical models and concepts using simulations to achieve a model with perfect goodness of fit. The results of the current study concluded that (1) the senior foreign tourists are sensitive to the issues of environmental pollution, air and water pollution, and social and cultural change, which require destination managers to closely consider these issues; and (2) the dominant respondents in this study are repeat visitors who are knowledgeable on the development and changes in Bali as a tourism destination.

3.6.2 *Recommendations*

Maintaining the use of a combined approach (mixed methods) is essential because this approach was able to address issues that are not sufficiently answered by quantitative approach alone. However, one thing to be improved is the selection real indicators that truly represent the latent variables, by first conducting unidimensionality analysis on all indicators before conducting field research so that the indicators are perfectly reliable to the latent variables.

This advice is intended for stakeholders involved to be able to use these results as a secondary data, in order to fit the variety of needs, desires, and expectations of senior tourists visiting Bali. Some respondents argued that the uniqueness of Balinese culture has experienced a decline with the rise of construction boom and tourism facilities, including hotels offering various types of accommodation that are not in accordance to the unique physical characteristics of Balinese culture; therefore, the government should make binding rules and policies to preserve the physical characteristics of Balinese culture and architecture.

Addressing the problem of waste, traffic congestion, and immigration services, these factors are considered less than optimum for a world-class travel destination. Also, the number of charges and retributions outside the inclusive tourists' budget, the building and development of tourism facilities with distinct Balinese cultural and architectural influences, and reduction in the use of materials derived from plastic are some programs that should be prioritized by Bali tourism policy makers and practitioners.

The next suggestion is intended for all segments and levels of society, on the need to preserving the image of Bali as a world-class tourism destination that has been perceived as good in the perspective of senior foreign tourists visiting Bali. This perceived image includes: (1) Bali as a tourism destination is considered to have a unique culture, (2) Bali as a tourism destination is considered to have friendly local population, (3) Bali is considered to have a complete tourism infrastructure, and (4) Bali as a tourism destination is considered to have a comfortable atmosphere for traveling.

References

Beerli A, Martin JD (2004) Factors influencing destination image. Ann Tour Res 31(3):657–681

Chi G (2005) A study of developing destination loyalty model. (Dissertation). The Faculty of the Graduate College of the Oklahoma State University in Partial Fulfillment of the Requirements for the Degree of Doctor of Philosophy, Oklahoma, July 2005

Cohen E (1984) The sociology of tourism: approaches, issues and findings. Ann Rev Soc 10:373–392

Dimanche F, Havitz ME (1994) Consumer behavior and tourism: review and extension of four study areas. J Travel Tour Mark 3(3):37–58

Esichaikul R (2012) Travel motivations, behavior and requirements of European senior tourists to Thailand. Sukhothai. J Thammathirat Open Univ Thail 10(2, Special Issue):47–58

Ferdinand A (2002) Structural equation modeling Dalam Penelitian Manajemen. BP UNDIP, Semarang

Flavian C, Martinez E, Polo Y (2001) Loyalty to Grocery Stores in the Spanish Market of the 1990s. J Retail Consum Serv 8:85–93

Hu YZ, Ritchie JRB (1993) Measuring destination attractiveness: a contextual approach. J Travel Res 32(2):25–34

Iso-Ahola SE (1991) Sightseeing tourists' motivation and satisfaction. Ann Tour Res 18(2):226–237

Kotler P (2003) Manajemen Pemasaran, Analisis Perencanaan, Implementasi dan kontrol. Prehalindo, Jakarta

Kozak M, Rimmington M (2000) Tourist satisfaction with Mallorca, Spain, as an off-season holiday destination. J Travel Res 38(3):260–269

Milman A, Pizam A (1995) The role of awareness and familiarity with a destination: the central florida case. J Travel Res 33(3):21–27

Oliver RL (1999) When customer loyalty. J Mark 63(Special Issues):33–34

Patterson I (2006) Growing older: tourism and leisure behaviour of older adults. School of tourism and leisure management, CABI is a Trading Name of CAB International: University of Queensland, Australia

Pitana IG, Gayatri PG (2005) Sosiologi Pariwisata. Penerbit Andi, Yogyakarta

Setiawan B (2002) Kesadaran dan Kepedulian Lansia. Cited Februari 17, 2010. Available from http://www.depsos.go.id

Som APM, Badarneh MB (2011) Tourist satisfaction and repeat visitation; toward a new comprehensive model. Int J Hum Soc Sci 6(1):2011

United Nation-World Tourism Organization (WTO) (2005) Tourism highlight UNWTO: international tourist arrivals, Tourism barometer 12: World Tourism Organization (UNWTO) Calle Capitán Haya, 42 28020 Madrid, Spain

Uysal M, Hagan LR (1993) Motivation of pleasure to travel and tourism. In: Khan MA, Olsen MD, Var T (eds) VNR'S encyclopedia of hospitality and tourism. Van Nostrand Reinhold, New York

Yoon Y, Muzaffer U (2003) An examination of the effects of motivation and satisfaction on destination loyalty: a structural model. Tourism Management. Virginia Polytechnic Institute and State University, Blacksburg (in press)

Zeithaml VA, Bitner MJ (2000) Services marketing. McGraw-Hill International Editions, Singapore

I. Gusti Bagus Rai Utama is a lecturer at Dhyana Pura University, Jl. Raya Padang Luwih, Dalung, Kuta Utara, Badung, Bali, Indonesia. He earned a PhD in Tourism (2014) from Udayana University, Bali, Indonesia; Master's Degree in Leisure and Tourism Studies (2007), CHN, Leeuwarden, Netherlands; Master's Degree in Agribusiness Management (2005), Udayana University, Bali Indonesia; and Bachelor of Economics in Economic Development (2001), Mahasaraswati University, Bali, Indonesia. Research interests are in Economics for Tourism and Leisure, Wellness Tourism and Tourism for senior, and Destination Economics.

Chapter 4
Hedonic Shopping Motivation: Does It Really Matter?

Tjong Budisantoso, Abhishek Bhati, Adrian Bradshaw, and Chun Meng Tang

Abstract In this chapter we intend to investigate the relationship between hedonic shopping motivation, shopping experience and retail outcome. The study is conducted in Surabaya, Indonesia. Three hundred and thirty shoppers participated in the study. The study found significant relationship between interior and layout and adventure motivation, interior and layout and social motivation, social factor and social motivation and social factor and idea motivation, service quality and interior and layout and social factor, shopping satisfaction and service quality and repatronage intention and shopping satisfaction.

Keywords Hedonic shopping motivation • Social motivation • Shopping satisfaction • Store layout

4.1 Introduction

Retailers believe that store atmosphere could influence purchasing behaviour. The evidence shows that most retailers in the country put significant amount of investment on store atmosphere. The literature also provides strong support on the relationship between store atmosphere and purchasing behaviour. However, the body of literature on shopping motivation reveals a lack of empirical findings as to how hedonic shopping motivation influences the shoppers' in-store experience in terms of their perception of store atmosphere and their cognitive responses.

The understanding on hedonic shopping motivation is very important right now as a lot of shoppers look for the entertainment aspect of shopping. In the retail context, Arnold and Reynolds (2003) stress that 'hedonic shopping motives are similar to the task orientation of utilitarian shopping motives, only the task is

T. Budisantoso (✉) • A. Bhati • A. Bradshaw • C.M. Tang
Department of Business, James Cook University, Singapore, Singapore
e-mail: budisantoso.tjong@jcu.edu.au

P. Mandal, J. Vong (eds.), *Development of Tourism and the Hospitality Industry in Southeast Asia*, Managing the Asian Century,
DOI 10.1007/978-981-287-606-5_4

concerned with hedonic fulfilment, such as experiencing fun, amusement, fantasy and sensory stimulation' (p. 78). This study intends to investigate how hedonic shopping motivation influences the perception of store atmosphere, how the cognitive response is affected by store atmosphere and how the cognitive response affects retail outcomes. The study is conducted in Surabaya, Indonesia.

4.2 Background

People's goals are directed to the fulfilment of needs and wants. 'Need' refers to human requirements, generally physiological needs such as food, water or clothing (Schiffman and Kanuk 1997, p. 92). Since the 1920s, researchers have tried to classify human needs. Starch, for example, classified human needs in terms of 44 separate motives in 1923. Maslow's Hierarchy of Motivation, which is probably the best known classification, identified five distinct needs. Other theorists have provided different classifications, e.g. a trio of needs and a set of 20 psychogenic needs. What is clear from this is that needs are a difficult thing to classify.

Likewise, the 'need' for a particular product is often difficult to classify. For example, people buy a pizza because they feel hungry. But why would they prefer to purchase a pizza rather than something else? Needs may develop as acquired needs and wants (Schiffman and Kanuk 1997, p. 92). Acquired needs are a result of what we experience in our daily lives, such as the need for esteem, prestige, affection, power or learning. Wants are 'the expression of needs in actual situations' (Schiffman and Kanuk 1997, p. 92). These needs and wants can become goals which influence behaviour.

People may go to the store to achieve some of their goals. The literature defines a number of shopping typologies which reflect various goals based on particular variables (see Stone 1954; Stephenson and Willet 1969; Darden and Reynolds 1971; Darden and Ashton 1974; Moschis 1976; Williams et al. 1978; Bellenger and Korgaonkar 1980; Westbrook and Black 1985; Bloch et al. 1994; Reynolds et al. 2002; Rohm and Swaminathan 2002; Guiot and Roux 2010; Yang and Kim 2012).

For example, Stone (1954) provides a shopper's taxonomy based on the orientation of shoppers towards the activity of shopping. According to this taxonomy, shoppers could be broken into four types: (1) the economic consumer, (2) the personalising consumer, (3) the ethical consumer and (4) the apathetic consumer. The economic shopper approaches shopping from an economic perspective, which emphasises merchandise assortment, the product price and quality. The personalising consumer prefers to have a personal relationship with the seller. Shoppers who place more emphasis on the ethical value are called ethical consumers. Lastly, the apathetic shopper does not have an intrinsic interest in shopping.

Table 4.1 below provides a summary of typologies that have been identified by various researchers.

Another approach utilised to classify shopping typology is the motivation factor. A survey of the literature reveals there are only a few motivation-based shopper

Table 4.1 Shopper typologies

No.	Author and date	Shopper types
1.	Stone (1954)	1. Economic
		2. Personalising
		3. Ethical
		4. Apathetic
2.	Chicago Tribune (1955)	1. Dependent
		2. Compulsive
		3. Individualistic
3.	Stephenson and Willet (1969)	1. Store loyal
		2. Compulsive or recreational
		3. Convenience
		4. Price or bargain conscious
4.	Darden and Reynolds (1971)	1. Economic
		2. Personalising
		3. Moralistic
		4. Apathetic
5.	Tauber (1972)	*Personal motives*
		1. Role playing
		2. Diversion
		3. Self-gratification
		4. Learning about new trends
		5. Physical activity
		6. Sensory stimulation
		Social motives
		1. Social experiences outside home
		2. Communication with others
		3. Peer group attraction
		4. Affiliation
		5. Power and authority
		6. Stimulation
5.	Darden and Ashton (1974)	1. Quality oriented
		2. Fastidious
		3. Convenience
		4. Stamp collectors
		5. Stamp avoiders
		6. Apathetic
6.	Moschis (1976)	1. Store loyal
		2. Brand loyal
		3. Special shoppers
		4. Psychosocialising
		5. Name conscious
		6. Problem solving

(continued)

Table 4.1 (continued)

No.	Author and date	Shopper types
7.	Williams et al. (1978)	1. Low price
		2. Convenience
		3. Involved
		4. Apathetic
8.	Bellenger and Korgaonkar (1980)	1. Recreational
		2. Economic
9.	Bloch et al. (1994)	1. Enthusiasts
		2. Traditionalists
		3. Grazers
		4. Minimalists
10.	Westbrook and Black (1985)	1. Utility
		2. Economic
		3. Price discount
		4. Merchandise choice
		5. Affiliation
		6. Exercise power and authority
		7. Sensory stimulation
11.	Reynolds et al. (2002)	1. Basic
		2. Apathetic
		3. Destination
		4. Enthusiast
		5. Serious
		6. Brand seekers
12.	Arnold and Reynolds (2003)	1. Adventure shopping
		2. Social shopping
		3. Gratification shopping
		4. Idea shopping
		5. Role shopping
		6. Value shopping

typologies. Amongst these are those developed by Tauber (1972), Westbrook and Black (1985) and Arnold and Reynolds (2003). Tauber's shopping typology reveals the non-product acquired motive. Westbrook and Black (1985) developed a comprehensive shopping typology based on motivation variables. More recently, Arnold and Reynolds (2003) extend the literature by investigating hedonic shopping motivation.

Tauber (1972) conducted an exploratory study to uncover the reasons why people shop. The sample used in the study, both men and women, was quite different to samples used in previous studies such as those of Stone (1954) and the Chicago Tribune (1955). These two studies focused solely on females. By including men in the sample, the study findings may have been enriched.

The most interesting finding from Tauber's study was the recognition of non-product motives. Tauber stressed that 'an understanding of shopping motives requires the consideration of satisfactions which shopping activities provide, as well as the utility obtained from the merchandise that may be purchased' (p. 58). This view provides a new insight on shopping typology.

Specifically, Tauber's typology is divided into two main categories (pp. 47–48). The first category, personal motives, consists of:

1. *Role playing*. This motive relates to the role of the shopper in the society. Housewives tend to view grocery shopping as one of their roles in society.
2. *Diversion*. Some people use shopping as a recreational activity.
3. *Self-gratification*. In this case shopping is seen as a medium for expressing different emotional states or moods.
4. *Learning about new trends*. Finding information about new products and model provides motivation for some people to go to the store.
5. *Physical activity*. Going shopping is an alternative for doing exercise.
6. *Sensory stimulation*. Some shoppers go to the store in order to gain some sensory benefit.

The second category of shopping motive category is social:

1. *Social experiences outside the home*. Shopping is viewed as a medium for socialising.
2. *Communication with others having a similar interest*. Some people go shopping for the opportunity to interact with others having similar interests.
3. *Peer group attraction*. Shopping is a way to self-express, to be with one's peer group or a reference group.
4. *Status and authority*. Some people go shopping to gain attention and respect.
5. *The pleasure of bargaining*. Shopping brings pleasure through bargaining over the price.

A later study by Westbrook and Black (1985) concluded that motivation-based shopping typology is the most appropriate way to classify shoppers. This framework is viewed as guiding retail strategy formulation as well as advancing efforts to develop more comprehensive theories of shopping behaviour. In addition, 'the consideration of motivation is implicit in extant typologies' (Westbrook and Black 1985, p. 35).

Westbrook and Black's shopping typology is as follows (pp. 86–87):

(a) *Anticipated utility*. Some people go to the store with the aim of obtaining a particular product. They expect to gain the utility offered by that product.
(b) *Role enactment*. The idea of this shopping motivation is arguably similar to role playing in Tauber's shopping typology. The motive for going to the store is largely affected by the person's role in society, which is culturally defined.
(c) *Negotiation*. Some people gain satisfaction if they can negotiate the price, believing they gain a good value product. Tauber (1972) named this motive as the pleasure of bargaining.

(d) *Choice optimisation*. For some people, shopping is a way to find a suitable product to fulfil their need.
(e) *Affiliation*. Socialising with other persons in the store is another shopper motivation. Westbrook and Black (1985) added the term of indirect affiliation, to express the intention to interact with a particular group. This idea encompasses three of the motives in Tauber's shopping typology: social experiences outside the home, communication with others having similar interests and peer group attraction.
(f) *Power and authority*. Shopping for some people is seen as a means of improving their social position.
(g) *Stimulation*. Some people go to the store with the main purpose of interacting with the store environment in order to feel stimulated. This shopping motive was also raised in Tauber's shopping typology.

As can be seen, although Westbrook and Black provided different norms and focused on motivation, many of their resulting categories are similar to those proposed by Tauber (1972).

The concept of hedonic shopping motivation is an extension of the concept of hedonic consumption (Hirschman and Holbrook 1982). Hirschman and Holbrook explained hedonic consumption as something that 'designates those facets of consumer behaviour that relate to the multisensory, fantasy and emotive aspects of one's experience with the product' (p. 92).

In the retail context, Arnold and Reynolds (2003) stress that 'hedonic shopping motives are similar to the task orientation of utilitarian shopping motives, only the task is concerned with hedonic fulfilment, such as experiencing fun, amusement, fantasy and sensory stimulation' (p. 78).

The hedonic shopping motivation typology developed by Arnold and Reynolds (2003, pp. 80–81) is as follows:

1. *Adventure shopping*. According to this motive, going shopping is an adventure. Arnold and Reynolds explain that people with this kind of motive expect to gain 'adventure, thrills, stimulation, excitement, and entering a different universe of exciting sights, smells, and sounds' (p. 80).
2. *Social shopping*. Socialising is the main purpose for some shoppers when they go shopping.
3. *Gratification shopping*. Life nowadays is so complex and the level of tension has increased in society. Some people go shopping to ease this tension.
4. *Idea shopping*. Shopping could update people's knowledge about the development of new trends and models.
5. *Role shopping*. Arnold and Reynolds highlight the concept of this motive by stating 'role shopping reflects the enjoyment that shoppers derive from shopping for others, the influence that this activity has on the shoppers' feeling and moods, and the excitement and intrinsic joy felt by shoppers when finding the perfect gift for others' (p. 81).
6. *Value shopping*. Some people go shopping to find a good value product.

Role shopping motivation relates to an individual's role in society, as explained before in Tauber's shopping typology and the Westbrook and Black (1985) motivation-based shopping typology. The main difference between these two typologies and the Arnold and Reynolds typology is that the former consider that shopping is part of their role in society. Arnold and Reynolds, however, posit that besides gaining satisfaction from fulfilling their duty, shoppers also expect to gain personal satisfaction from buying something for other people.

Hedonic shopping motivation typology, including product acquisition motivation, is the main interest of this research. Most motivation typologies consider utilitarian and hedonic motivation because they are the underlying forces that drive all consumption (Babin et al. 1994). Babin and Attaway (2000, p. 3) differentiate utilitarian value as task-related worth and hedonic value as shopping-value worth for shoppers. These shopping motivations are hypothesised to influence in-store experience in terms of their perception of store atmosphere and their cognitive responses.

Hibbert and Tagg (2001) use the concept of goal-directed behaviour to explain the hypothesised relationship between shopping motivation and the experience of shopping.

According to Pervin (1987), this theory argues that 'there is an organized, persistent, directed quality to much of human behaviour and the concept of goal is suggested as a means for directing attention to, and understanding an aspect of human behaviour that transcends the immediacy of the particular situation or moment' (p. 228).

To study this theory, Heckhausen (1991, p. 183) differentiates the phases of goal-directed behaviour into (1) the 'pre-decisional phase', (2) the 'pre-actional phase', (3) the 'actional phase' and (4) the 'post-actional phase'. The pre-decisional phase is the situation when a person is confronted with alternative goals. A person has to decide which goal to pursue in order to allocate his or her effort or resources. In the pre-actional phase, a person develops a strategy or plan to pursue the goal. In the actional phase, a person acts to pursue the goal and evaluates the process. In the post-actional phase, the person evaluates whether he or she has attained the intended goal.

Motives can influence how people evaluate the product purchased (Lawson et al. 1996, p. 314). A utilitarian product such as a computer would generate more of a thinking process than a hedonic product. In contrast, hedonic products such as high fashion clothes would involve the hedonic experiences of product symbolism, physical and psychological stimulation.

In the retail setting, few studies have investigated the role of motivation. Dawson et al. (1990) found that shopping motivation could influence the emotions induced by the atmosphere of a store. Specifically, strongly product-motivated customers would experience higher pleasure, while strongly experientially motivated customers would experience higher arousal. The retail choice and preference are also influenced directly by shopping motivation (pp. 424–425).

4.3 Research Hypothesis

In the retail context, Arnold and Reynolds (2003) stress that 'hedonic shopping motives are similar to the task orientation of utilitarian shopping motives, only the task is concerned with hedonic fulfilment, such as experiencing fun, amusement, fantasy and sensory stimulation' (p. 78). The hedonic shopping motivation typology developed by Arnold and Reynolds consists of adventure, social, gratification, idea, role and value shopping motivations.

Baker (1986) has developed a store atmosphere classification which consists of ambience, design and social factors. Ambience factors are background features that may or may not be consciously perceived but that affect human senses. Design factors refer to features directly perceptible by consumers, such as aesthetics and functionality. Lastly, social factor refers to the people in the environment, that is, other customers and service personnel.

The theory of goal-directed behaviour (Pervin 1987) explains that goal could direct behaviour at particular situation. Different shopping motivations could lead to exploring different parts of store atmosphere.

H1 People with adventure shopping motivation would perceive store atmosphere more positively than people with other shopping motivations in Surabaya.
H2 People with social shopping motivation would perceive social factors more positively than people with other shopping motivations in Surabaya.
H3 People with idea shopping motivation inwould perceive social factors more positively than people with other shopping motivations in Surabaya.

The review of perceived service quality conceptions emphasises the importance of the influence of the physical environment on the perception of service quality. The SERVQUAL model (Parasuraman et al. 1988) includes the tangible component, representing physical evidence of the service. The three-component model identifies the service environment as one of the components in the model affecting the perceived service quality. The hierarchical model (Brady and Cronin 2001) takes account of physical environment quality. The perception of service quality and the perception of merchandise quality were also found to be antecedents to store image rather than components of the store image (Baker et al. 1994, pp. 332–3). Brocato et al. (2012)) emphasise on the importance of cues of other people in the service experience.

H4 Service quality associates with the perception on store atmosphere in Surabaya.

Literature reveals the relationship between perceived service quality and satisfaction as 'perceived service quality → satisfaction → behavioural intention'. According to this approach, the evaluation of service quality, which is cognitive in nature, may influence satisfaction, which in turn affects behavioural intention (Parasuraman et al. 1988). Rust and Oliver (1997) also explain that the perception of service quality is one dimension that influences satisfaction. Therefore, it is hypothesised that

H5 Store patronage satisfaction is affected by service quality in Surabaya.

Store patronage satisfaction has been found to influence store loyalty (Bloemer and de Ruyter 1998), word of mouth, price insensitivity, purchase intentions and complaint behaviour (Bloemer and Odekerken-Schroder 2002). Stoel et al. (2004) found that satisfaction with mall attributes is an antecedent for store repatronage intention.

H6 Repatronage intention is associated with the store patronage satisfaction in Surabaya.

4.4 The Survey Results

330 shoppers were recruited randomly to serve as subjects. The store environments chosen for the study are supermarkets, specialty stores and department stores. This study used measurement instruments developed by other researchers. Partial least square (PLS) was utilised to analyse the data.

Most of the respondents were aged 18–24 years old. This age group accounts for 61.2 % of the entire sample. The majority of respondents in Surabaya were accompanied by 1–3 people (82.1 %).

4.4.1 Exploratory Factor Analysis (EFA)

The factor analysis on shopping motivation in Surabaya reveals six factors. The factors identified are adventure, idea, social, role, value and product acquisition shopping motivation. Indonesian shoppers identify store atmosphere as interior layout, design factor, social factor and store attractiveness. In Surabaya, the factor analysis on cognitive responses yields two factors. However one factor is eliminated as the measurements do not have any meaning. The recognised factor could be identified as the perception of service quality. Furthermore, the factor analysis on store patronage satisfaction in Surabaya also yields two factors. The study concentrates on the first factor as it has most of the satisfaction concept measurement, while the second factor only comprises one measurement. The factor analysis on repatronage intention produces one factor. Accordingly, this factor is identified as repatronage intention.

4.4.2 Confirmatory Factor Analysis (CFA)

Measurement model. To assess the measurement model, internal consistency reliability (composite reliability > 0.7), indicator reliability (item loading > 0.7, significant at 0.05 level), convergent validity (average variance extracted (AVE) > 0.5) and

Table 4.2 CR, AVE and correlations of reflective constructs

Construct	CR	AVE	Adventure	Idea	Social	Interior	Socfac	Service	Satisfact	Repatron
Adventure	0.9	0.643	0.802	0.453	0.451	0.37	0.301	0.207	0.272	0.271
Idea	0.919	0.791	0.453	0.889	0.383	0.248	0.271	0.123	0.155	0.314
Social	0.87	0.691	0.451	0.383	0.831	0.368	0.335	0.231	0.298	0.249
Interior	0.922	0.702	0.37	0.248	0.368	0.838	0.688	0.354	0.512	0.4
Socfac	0.833	0.714	0.301	0.271	0.335	0.688	0.845	0.158	0.341	0.31
Service	0.885	0.721	0.207	0.123	0.231	0.354	0.158	0.849	0.66	0.419
Satisfact	0.887	0.663	0.272	0.155	0.298	0.512	0.341	0.66	0.814	0.513
Repatron	0.867	0.765	0.271	0.314	0.249	0.4	0.31	0.419	0.513	0.875

Note 1: Construct names to be confirmed

Note 2: CR: composite reliability. Internal consistency reliability is satisfactory when composite reliability is above 0.7

Note 3: AVE: average variance extracted. Convergent validity is considered satisfactory when the AVE is above 0.5

Note 4: Square roots of average variances extracted (AVE) are shown on diagonal. Correlations between constructs are shown on off-diagonal. Discriminant validity is satisfactory when square root of the AVE is larger than the correlations between constructs

discriminant validity (low cross-loadings on the unintended constructs and square root of the AVE is larger than the correlations between constructs) are examined (Urbach and Ahlemann 2010). Items of respective factors that had a loading of below 0.7 were excluded from the analysis. Tables 4.2 and 4.3 show the final assessment results of the reflective measurement model.

4.5 Structural Model Analysis

To assess the structural model, we examined R^2 (values around 0.670 are strong, 0.333 moderate and 0.190 weak), effect size (f^2, values around 0.02 are small, 0.15 medium and 0.35 large) and path coefficient in terms of sign, magnitude and significance. Figure 4.1 shows the results of the analysis:

The path coefficient between adventure and interior was significant ($\beta=0.29$, $p<0.01$, $f^2=0.12$).

The path coefficient between social and interior was significant ($\beta=0.28$, $p<0.01$, $f^2=0.11$).

The path coefficient between social and socfac was significant ($\beta=0.28$, $p<0.01$, $f^2=0.10$).

The path coefficient between idea and socfac was significant ($\beta=0.18$, $p<0.01$, $f^2=0.05$).

The path coefficient between interior and service was significant ($\beta=0.31$, $p<0.01$, $f^2=0.11$).

The path coefficient between socfac and service was insignificant ($\beta=-0.10$, $p=0.15$, $f^2=0.02$).

Table 4.3 Factor loadings and cross-loadings of reflective constructs

Construct/ Items/	Adventu	Idea	Social	Interio	Socfac	service	Satisfact	Repatro
Sadvsho	0.732	-0.101	0.079	-0.086	0.066	-0.046	-0.025	0.054
Sadvsho	0.849	-0.024	0.005	-0.06	0.033	0.038	-0.039	0.078
Sadvsho	0.808	0.076	-0.022	-0.039	-0.034	0.066	-0.139	-0.001
Sgrtsho	0.81	0.01	-0.016	0.057	-0.001	-0.061	0.203	-0.149
Sgrtsho	0.806	0.03	-0.04	0.124	-0.059	-0.004	0	0.019
Sidshop	-0.003	0.926	-0.054	-0.029	0.006	0.01	0.01	-0.06
Sidshop	0.034	0.936	0.002	-0.051	-0.001	-0.029	0.034	-0.043
Sidshop	-0.036	0.8	0.061	0.093	-0.006	0.022	-0.051	0.12
Ssoshop	0.046	-0.076	0.804	-0.009	-0.11	0.107	-0.193	0.157
Ssoshop	-0.079	0.008	0.884	-0.084	0.035	-0.071	0.076	0.012
Ssoshop	0.042	0.067	0.803	0.101	0.072	-0.03	0.109	-0.171
Design9	-0.054	0.015	-0.028	0.841	-0.065	0.081	-0.101	0.076
Ambient	0.012	0.03	0	0.908	0.032	-0.002	-0.028	0.056
Design8	-0.07	0.05	0.088	0.848	0.128	0.059	-0.143	-0.024
Ambient	0.024	-0.085	-0.101	0.777	-0.246	0.041	0.046	-0.116
Social2	0.093	-0.02	0.034	0.81	0.133	-0.183	0.243	-0.006
Social1	0.117	-0.129	-0.088	-0.066	0.845	-0.04	0.17	0.109
Design2	-0.117	0.129	0.088	0.066	0.845	0.04	-0.17	-0.109
InSerQu	-0.074	0.004	0.042	0.197	-0.05	0.895	0.093	-0.048
InSerQu	-0.057	0.068	-0.015	0.009	-0.004	0.877	-0.061	-0.015
InSerQu	0.151	-0.082	-0.033	-0.24	0.062	0.769	-0.04	0.072
Satisfact	0.067	-0.021	0.043	0.06	0.082	-0.05	0.805	0.068
Satisfact	-0.032	0.048	0.03	-0.186	0.04	0.148	0.832	-0.182
Satisfact	0.043	-0.037	-0.038	-0.004	0.047	-0.205	0.786	0.085
Satisfact	-0.074	0.007	-0.035	0.132	-0.163	0.094	0.833	0.036
Repint2	0.005	0.072	-0.025	0.111	-0.088	-0.139	0.155	0.875
Repint3	-0.005	-0.072	0.025	-0.111	0.088	0.139	-0.155	0.875

Note 1: Construct names to be confirmed
Note 2: All item loadings are significant at 0.01 level. Indicator reliability is considered satisfactory when item loadings are > 0.7, significant at 0.05 level
Note 3: Discriminant validity is considered satisfactory when items exhibit high loadings on the intended constructs (>0.5) and low cross-loadings on the unintended constructs

The path coefficient between service and satisfact was significant ($\beta = 0.66, p < 0.01, f^2 = 0.44$).

The path coefficient between satisfact and repatron was significant ($\beta = 0.51, p < 0.01, f^2 = 0.27$).

The constructs adventure and social explained about 23 % of the variance of interior. The constructs social and idea explained about 15 % of the variance of socfac. The constructs socfac and interior explained about 10 % of the variance of service. The construct service explained about 44 % of the variance of satisfact. The construct satisfact explained about 26 % of the variance of repatron.

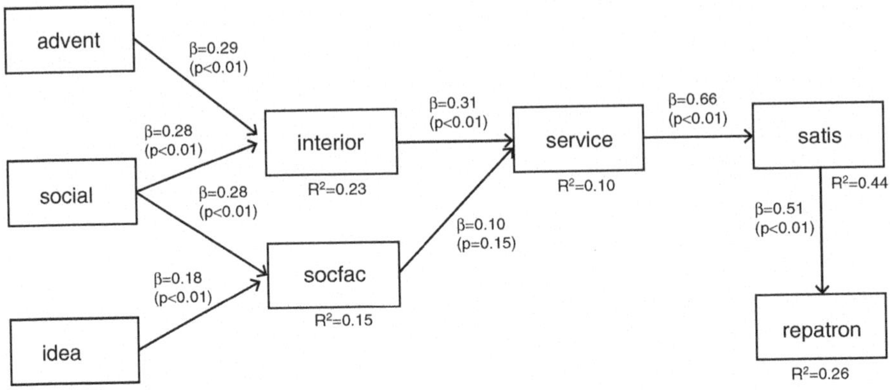

Fig. 4.1 Results of PLS analysis

4.6 Conclusion

The study results suggest that adventure motivation associates with interior layout; social motivation affects interior layout, and social factor and idea motivation associates with social factor in Surabaya. In the retail context, shopping goals can direct attention and influence behaviour. In addition, most motivation definitions emphasise that motivation is an important influence on people's actions (Lawson et al. 1996).

The perception of service quality has a positive association with interior layout and social factors. The findings of this study in Surabaya support this definition of perceived service quality in terms of the customer-employee interaction and physical environment. In addition, Parasuraman et al.'s (1988) SERVQUAL model includes the tangible component to represent physical evidence of the service.

Store patronage satisfaction associates with the perception of service quality in Surabaya. The emergence of the perception of service as the most important variable to influence satisfaction is reasonably acceptable. This study also confirms the relationship between repatronage intention and store patronage satisfaction.

4.7 Future Trends

As the research findings indicate that hedonic shopping goals are an important factor to influence the perception of store atmosphere, retailers should consider this factor when designing store atmosphere. Retailers should consider hedonic shopper goals when designing all store atmosphere components: interior layout, design factors, social factors and store attractiveness. For example, in relation to interior layout, retailers should have a well-organised layout and an impressive interior in order to enhance a response from adventure and social motivation shoppers.

The perception of service quality relates to store atmosphere particularly interior layout and social factors. Therefore, to develop a superior service quality perception, retailers should emphasise social factors and interior layout.

This finding suggests that store patronage satisfaction is influenced by service quality at the store. Therefore, retailers should increase the perception of service quality in order to increase store patronage satisfaction. This satisfaction can, in turn, increase shoppers' repatronage intentions.

References

Arnold MJ, Reynolds KE (2003) Hedonic shopping motivation. J Retail 79(2):79

Babin BJ, Attaway JS (2000) Atmospheric affect as a tool for creating value and gaining share of customer. J Bus Res 49:91–99

Babin BJ, Darden WR, Griffin M (1994) Work and/or fun: measuring hedonic and utilitarian shopping value. J Consum Res 20:644–656

Baker J (1986) The role of the environment in marketing services: the consumer perspective. In: Czepiel JA, Congram CA, Shanahan J (eds) The services challenge: integrating for competitive advantage. American Marketing Association, Chicago, pp 79–84

Baker J, Grewal D, Parasuraman A (1994) The influence of store environment on quality interferences and store image. J Acad Mark Sci 27:84–204

Bellenger DN, Korgaonkar PK (1980) Profiling the recreational shopper. J Retail 56:3

Bloch PH, Ridgway NM, Dawson SA (1994) The shopping mall as a consumer habitat. J Retail 70(1):23

Bloemer J, de Ruyter K (1998) On the relationship between store image, store satisfaction and store loyalty. Eur J Mark 32(5):499–513

Bloemer J, Odekerken-Schroder G (2002) Store satisfaction and store loyalty explained by customer- and store-related factors. J Consumer Satisf Dissatisf Complain Behav 15

Brady MK, Cronin JJ (2001) Some new thoughts on conceptualizing perceived service quality: a hierarchical approach. J Mark 65(3):34–39

Brocato ED, Voorhees CM, Baker J (2012) Understanding the influence of cues from other customers in the service experience: a scale development and validation. J Retail 88(3):384–398

Darden WR, Ashton D (1974) Psychographic profiles of patronage preference groups. J Retail 50(winter):99–112

Darden WR, Reynolds FD (1971) Shopping orientations and product usage roles. J Mark Res 8:505–508

Dawson S, Bloch PH, Ridgway NM (1990) Shopping motives, emotional states and retail outcomes. J Retail 66(4):408–427

Guiot D, Roux D (2010) A second-hand shoppers' motivation scale: antecedents, consequences, and implications for retailers. J Retail 86(4):355–371

Heckhausen H (1991) Motivation and action. Springer, Berlin

Hibbert S, Tagg SK (2001) Shopping motivation: investigating the shopping process and outcomes of the retail experience at a craft fair. J Mark Manag 17:341

Hirschman EC, Holbrook MB (1982) Hedonic consumption: emerging concepts. J Market 46(summer):92–101

Lawson R, Tidwell P, Raibird P, Loudon D, Della Bitta A (1996) Consumer behaviour in Australia & New Zealand. McGraw-Hill, Brisbane

Moschis GP (1976) Shopping orientations and consumer uses of information. J Retail 52(summer):61–70

Parasuraman A, Zeithaml VA, Berry LA (1988) SERVQUAL: a multiple item scale for measuring consumer perceptions of service quality. J Retail 64(spring):12–37

Pervin LA (1987) Person-environment congruence in the light of person-situation controversy. J Vocat Behav 31(3):222

Reynolds KE, Ganesh J, Luckett M (2002) Traditional malls vs. factory outlets: comparing shopper typologies and implications for retail strategy. J Bus Res 55:687–696

Rohm AJ, Swaminathan V (2002) A typology of online shoppers based on shopping motivations. J Bus Res. Article in Press: 11

Rust RT, Oliver RL (1997) Service quality: insights and managerial implications from the retailer. In: Rust RT, Oliver RL (eds) Service quality: new directions in theory and practice. Sage Publications, New York

Schiffman LB, Kanuk W (1997) Consumer behaviour. Prentice Hall, Singapore

Stephenson RP, Willet RP (1969) Analysis of consumers' retail patronage strategies. In: McDonald PR (ed) Marketing involvement in society and the economy. American Marketing Association, Chicago, pp 316–322

Stoel L, Wickliffe V, Lee KH (2004) Attribute beliefs and spending as antecedents to shopping value. J Bus Res 57(10):1067–1073

Stone GP (1954) City shoppers and urban identification: observation on the social psychology of city life. Am J Sociol 60(July):36–45

Tauber EM (1972) Why do people shop? J Mark 36(October):46–59

Tribune C (1955) Psychological aspects of shopping: a supplement to the new consumer. Chicago Tribune Research Division, Chicago

Urbach N, Ahlemann F (2010) Structural equation modelling in information systems research using partial least squares. J Inf Technol Theory Appl 11(2)

Westbrook RA, Black WC (1985) A motivation-based shopper typology. J Retail 61(spring):78–103

Williams RH, Painter JJ, Herbert NR (1978) A policy-oriented typology of grocery shoppers. J Retail 54(spring):27–43

Yang K, Kim H (2012) Mobile motivation: an application of multiple discriminant analysis. Int J Retail Distrib Manag 40(10):778–789

Tjong Budisantoso is a lecturer of Marketing at James Cook University, Singapore campus. He received International Postgraduate Research Scholarship (IPRS) from the Australia Commonwealth Government in 2002. He has intensive researches in branding and retailing.

Bhati Abhishek is responsible for overseeing academic governance and administration and introducing strategies to enhance student experience for the College of Business, Law and Governance programmes offered in the Singapore campus. He has worked in the education industry with leading providers for more than 14 years. He is particularly interested in the impact of tourism on the economy as well as social sustainability. His PhD thesis studies tourist vandalism, motivation factors of a vandal's behaviour and effectiveness of stakeholder responses. His other projects include incorporating 'work integrated learning' (WIL)-based learning strategies in tertiary education. His recent project involved implementing WIL in university curriculum

Adrian Bradshaw is a lecturer at James Cook University, Singapore campus. His major research areas include IS evaluation, strategic IS, IS business alignment and digital innovation. He has received research grants, published journal papers and conference papers and book chapters as well as edited various books.

Chun Meng Tang is employed as a lecturer of Business at JCU, Singapore. He has a background in Computer Science and Physics and a career in information technology management, administration and support before attaining his PhD in Management. He has a keen interest in qualitative research and the application of qualitative methods to business management, knowledge management and information systems development.

Chapter 5
The SWOT Analysis of Turkish Airlines Through Skytrax Quality Evaluations in the Global Brand Process

Erkan Sezgin and Deniz Yuncu

Abstract Skytrax is a foundation which collects consumer evaluations/questionnaires of airlines, airports, airport lounges, cabin services and caterings, and air cabin crew in order to consolidate evaluations and scores airlines and airports from one star to five stars. Skytrax evaluations of both Turkish Airlines (TK) and Singapore Airlines (SQ) are compared in this particular study. The reason for such benchmarking is to identify the strengths and weaknesses of four-starred TK in contrast to distinguished and permanent five-starred SQ. Strengths, weaknesses, opportunities, and threats (SWOT) analysis is implemented on both airlines' Skytrax criteria, and results revealed that TK has significant weaknesses on three main topics which are "cleanliness," "staff presentation," and "handling delays/cancelations."

Keywords Skytrax • Branding • Airlines • Services quality • SWOT analysis

5.1 Introduction

It is generally agreed today that branding is the process of creating a slogan from a message and then designing a symbol or logo that goes together with the slogan which will communicate with potential visitors the image of the city along with the features, benefits, and values it has to offer. While the words and symbols used together are simply accepted as a brand, the term *brand name* actually refers to the

---

E. Sezgin, Ph.D. (✉)
Faculty of Tourism, Tour Guiding Department, Anadolu University,
Yunusemre Campus, 26470 Eskisehir, Turkey
e-mail: esezgin@anadolu.edu.tr

D. Yuncu, Ph.D.
Faculty of Tourism, Tourism Mangement Department, Anadolu University,
Yunusemre Campus, 26470 Eskisehir, Turkey
e-mail: dkaragoz@anadolu.edu.tr

P. Mandal, J. Vong (eds.), *Development of Tourism and the Hospitality Industry in Southeast Asia*, Managing the Asian Century,
DOI 10.1007/978-981-287-606-5_5

words, while the term *brand mark* refers to the symbol or logo (Kolb 2006). Reducing consumer purchase risk, building awareness by communicating a consistent message, encouraging repeat visits by building consumer loyalty, and associating the city with a unique identity are common benefits of branding. Souvenirs are tangible evidence of where the traveler has been and when displayed at home, will inform others about their values and identity (Caldwell and Freire 2004). As a result of globalization and horizontal integration all over the world, companies have been seeking branding with the intent of recognition, and airline companies are not the exceptions.

Building a strong brand has been one of the most popular marketing efforts for any company nowadays. The airlines that survive in the battle for the market share may be attributed to the ones that build a strong brand and influence by engaging consumers within their brand and improve value (Sezgin and Kozak 2012). The value of a strong brand has been more important than ever. At the same time, influencing in a community creates powerful leverage for strong brands (Brymer 2009).

The Skytrax brand is recognized and associated with quality excellence throughout the world by the air transport industry, and Skytrax has become well known among the traveling public with the airline star rating, World Airline Awards, and World Airport Awards (www.airlinequality.com).

Turkish Airlines (TK) has been a remarkable example of such successful companies in the process. Having been established in 1933 as "Star Airlines Administration" and restructured as "Turkish Airlines" in 1955, the airline has celebrated its 75th foundation anniversary in 2008 (Turkish Airlines gears up to enhance market share 2008). In 2008, TK became a member of Star Alliance which is one of the largest airline alliances in the world. In order to build and keep alive its brand equity, which provides a serious advantage in terms of competition, TK has also focused on the investments that support the brand equity (Sezgin and Kozak 2012), that is to say, offering quality of presentation and investing in highly qualified personnel (Mechtronix Ascent and Trainer 2010). As a result of all the above mentioned efforts, the company was declared to be one the four most profitable airlines in the world, carrying 22.53 million passengers with its fleet of 130 aircraft in 2008 (Why's Turkish the atypical Middle Eastern airline brand? 2010).

Today, TK, which is one of the major brands in the airline industry, is an accurate representation of Turkey and is also increasing securely in a right way toward branding. Singapore Airlines (SQ), on the other hand, is a successful and powerful competitor which TK benchmarks in its operations. TK assigns successful logo and symbol for branding process by using traditional Turkish rose and tulip are the motifs on the first and business class tickets. More importantly, the company continues with another *brand identity* creating component nowadays: slogans. TK for the last 4 years (including 2014) has been chosen as Europe's best airline by Skytrax provider. Having the title, the company uses the slogan: "the best flies with Europe's best airline." On the other hand, TK has introduced the fragrance "TK 1933" to use as a tool to take the airline's brand to another level. The fragrance is intended to provide a sensory recognition of the global branding of TK and to bring a sense of relaxation and happiness (www.airlinequality.com).

This study particularly investigates the strengths and weaknesses of TK in global branding process as well as opportunities and threats. A distinguished airline company, SQ was chosen as benchmark since the company is accepted as best in class (BIC) (Erturk 2011) by many authorities in the air transportation industry. Moreover, SQ is a kind of "permanent five-star airline" in the Skytrax list for years.

5.2 Literature Review

In general sense, transportation is a process or relocation of assets from one place to another. The concept of air transportation is to carry people and goods (cargo, baggage, mail) by air (Çelik 2012). The main task of the service enterprises the marketing direction, to plan and develop the appropriate services to the market. The aim of the airline business is to meet the needs of passengers; in-flight cabin services, ticketing, baggage transfer services, and cargo services are all the services provided (Okumuş and Asil 2007). After collecting all the necessary information about the market, the marketing strategy must be determined (Okumuş and Asil 2007). The marketing environment, however, is becoming more competitive, as the international market is expanding and airlines are returning to profit after the recession in the early 1990s (Betts 1994). Many developments have been technologically pushed: larger aircraft have increased capacity, leading to reduced real fares and many improved aspects of the in-flight experience (though the tendency to larger aircraft might now be ended (Skapinker 1995); computer reservation systems have simplified flight booking; airport infrastructure investment improved the preflight and postflight aspects of travel; computer systems managed reservations and yields; and investment in air traffic control systems and flight navigation systems improved the punctuality of airlines (Driver 1999).

Air transport is a lightly complex system consisting of interlinking distributed network made up of human operators, procedures, and technological systems. Furthermore, transportation itself is a service-based industry, and naturally service industries are affected by many variables during their operations. Airlines working hard on brand image and even the ones that already have had a prominent brand image could suffer easily after a hijacking attempt or an air traffic accident (Sezgin and Kozak 2012). Hence, brand performance can be defined as the relative measurement of the brand's success in the marketplace (Cass and Ngo 2007). Branding has been such a hot topic issue that affects many industries as well as destinations either on a regional level or on a national level. Lately in the tourism industry, destination branding has been a specific discipline; however, the tourism conglomerates did not pay sufficient attention on branding in the 1970s and 1980s, but they preferred more vertical integration with several brands and several sectors. However, the trend has turned out to horizontal integrations since the globalization process forced companies, as well as countries and union of countries, to integrate into one single brand under the same business sector (Sezgin 2008).

One of the most important issues in the airline business is the services provided by the airlines. Determining the needs of targeted consumers, airline companies should focus on before-, during-, and after-flight services. Services in airlines, cabin layout, the flight network, aircraft types and frequency of flights, ticket sales points, reservations, terminal services, punctuality, and flight are all classified as the services offered by airlines (Alkoç 2004).

5.2.1 Brand and Airline Industry

Both consumers and companies find brand and branding more important today. Perceived as identities by consumers, brands alert their senses as well as enrich their life experiences. People have a need to affiliate and surround themselves with things they know well, trust, and aspire to be. From the point of consumers, brand is a quality sign providing reliability between companies and consumers.

Etymologically, the Italian word "marca" consists of both signing and signalizing meanings. The symbols formed by figures and letters and metals used for tickets or coins are all named as brands. On the other hand, the word "branding" etymologically comes from the British peasants' purpose for separating cattle. Accordingly, the word branding means signing the items both for signalizing and distinguishing.

Brand is a name, term, design, symbol, or any other feature that identifies one seller's good or service as distinct from those of other sellers according to the American Marketing Association (AMA) (www marketingpower com 2999). Kotler (2001) defines brand as a seller's promise to deliver a specific set of features, benefits, and services consistent to the buyers (Kotler 2001). Aekar, another branding expert, finally describes it as the following: "brand is a defining and distinguishing name or symbol of seller's or group of seller's products and services from the competitors." Accordingly, the brand signalizing the source of product protects both consumers and producers from the potential competitors (Elitok 2003).

Companies in today's fierce competitive world are trying hard to brand their products. If recognition leads to increased sales of products/services, "brand recognition" is the most effective way for it. Brand is a promise of producers to consumers (Onan 2006). Brand provides a seller's or producer's service, characteristic, or advantage with permanent quality warranty, and this is not necessarily perceived the same by all consumers (Cop and Bekmezci 2005). The brand encourages pleased consumers to prefer the same product and to be "repeat buyers." Brand is a bridge between sellers and consumers; thus, consumers buy products/services from sellers through brand reliability. On the other hand, selling product is not the end of the process. After-sales services play an important role on brand image and brand loyalty. Consumers do not want to buy a no-name product which could be ruined easily after sale.

Brand is not only a registration certificate distinguishing products from the others but also a promise to consumers for permanent quality and performance. Symbolizing the advantages and quality of products/services, brand also contributes for "brand recall."

The branding attempts of airline companies have to be in collaboration with the strategies such as networking, job training, and fleet policy. The other two important strategies – the "on-time performance" and "value for money" – also have to be cohesive with branding (Taneja 2014). Branding is an important marketing instrument and it is more important to airline business compared to other businesses. It is impossible to see any single passenger airline in "the top 100 Global Brands." Relatively well-known airlines could argue with such lists and point out that such rankings have been based on brand equity and the market capitalizations of the global airlines tend to be relatively small. Other arguments include factors that although they are global in operations, airlines are not considered global business due to the existence of bilateral and multilateral agreements. These are valid explanations (Taneja). One of the basic conditions of sustainable competitive advantage is branding for the industries, and the airline industry is not an exception. Although it may vary through industries, brand loyalty of consumers is affected by several factors. Service quality is one of the most important factors in service industries (Zeithaml et al. 1996). Moreover, the service quality is a predecessor for brand loyalty, brand recognition, and brand satisfaction. Consequently, the marketing professionals try to identify "perceived quality" while defining the term brand. Professionals believe that consumers find high-quality products more successful when all other variables are considered as equals. Relatively, the brand quality definitions will strongly affect brand preferences (Morton 1994). Consequently, the marketing professionals claim that the service quality is a strong founder of the brand loyalty (Gremler et al. 1996). Tam (2000) and Chinomona et al. (2003) also support that service quality affects brand satisfaction directly.

5.2.2 *Service Quality*

Various researchers have tried to identify and conceptualize service quality in the areas of marketing and management. The first conceptual explanations (Grönroos et al. 1984) were based on the disconfirmation paradigm depending on the literature developed on the quality of physical goods and products. The perceived service quality can be defined as attitudes or judgments related to superiority of a service. Grönroos (2007) assumes that customers' perceived service quality is an output of the evaluation process in which customers compare their expectations with the actual service performance. By this logic, service quality is evaluated in two dimensions: the first dimension is technical quality, defined as a result of the interaction of customers with the service provider, and the other dimension is functional quality related to the given service (Grönroos 2007).

Parasuraman, Berry, and Zeithaml (1985) defined the concept of service quality as a discrepancy level between customers' normative service expectations and their perceptions of the service performance. The dominant theory in conceptualizing the phenomena of service quality and satisfaction is the paradigm of expectation-disconfirmation. This paradigm is composed of two processes: the first is the development of the output (result) expectations and the second is the confirmation/disconfirmation judgments arising from the comparison of the results perceived as contrary to these expectations. When the actual performance matches with the previous expectations, a match occurs. When the performance exceeds the expectations or when it occurs at a lower level, a negative or positive disconfirmation occurs. While negative mismatch causes a perception of low service quality or dissatisfaction, positive mismatch causes a perception of high level of service quality and satisfaction.

The airline sector is classified as one of the most abstract service sectors. The main reason for this classification is that it is a sector that has all of the distinctive features of services of the airline sector listed as abstractness, inseparability, unstableness, and instability (Clemes et al. 2008). The airline sector, having both labor-intensive and capital-intensive structures, can be affected very easily by economic, political, and social events because of its wide region in which it operates and it being an international business (Air Transport Association of America 2007). Today a lot of factors such as increased competition, prevention of governments from subsidizing the airline companies losing money, deregulation, etc., have been forcing the airline companies that want to survive to be more productive and more competitive (Aircraft Aerodynamics and Design Group Stanford University 2011). Because of high costs, it is very difficult for the airline enterprises operating with lower profit margins to compete with their competitors in terms of price in the long run. In addition, the competitor enterprises' reaction to price changes in a short time has led the airline enterprises to the area of service quality (Liou and Tzeng 2007).

Elliott and Roach (Elliot and Roach 1993) used the criteria of performance, baggage handling, food quality, seat comfort, check-in service, and flight service to evaluate the service performance of an airport. Ostrowski et al. (Ostrowski et al. 1993) evaluated the service quality in terms of punctuality, food and drink quality, and seat comfort. Chang and Yeh (2002) developed a fuzzy multi-criteria model to evaluate the service quality of local passenger airlines in Taiwan. Similarly, Liou et al. (2011) determined eight criteria in order to evaluate the service quality of domestic flights in Taiwan and to determine and develop their weak sides. The dimensions of their study are reservation services, ticketing services, check-in procedures, baggage handling, boarding process, cabin services, baggage claims, and responsiveness On the other hand, evaluation criteria for Taiwan Airlines are demonstrated in Table 5.1.

There are several criteria developed by various researchers in evaluating the quality of service offered in airline enterprises. There are criteria that have been developed by various institutions and organizations as well. Among them, one of the best-known criteria is Skytrax.

5.3 Case Study: Turkish Airlines (TK)

TK was established in 1933 as "the State Airlines Administration" belonging to the Ministry of National Defense. The first budget of the institution was 180 thousand liras, and it had a total of 24 staff, including seven pilots, eight mechanics, eight civil servants, and a radio operator. The first fleet consisted of two King Birds (five seats), two Junkers F 13 (four seats), and one ATH-9 (10 seats). In 1955, the name "General Directorate of State Airlines" was abolished with Law No. 6623, and it was named as Turkish Airlines, its present name. From 1955 until the 1980s, various activities were continued to develop the fleet and flight line of the Turkish Airlines. In the early 1980s, change and transformation projects began in Turkish Airlines, and these change and transformation projects were continued even in the 1990s. In the 2000s, there began a period of a major recession in aviation after the 9/11 attacks occurred in the United States. Because the economic crisis that started in those years had negative effects on Turkey, the years 2000 and 2001 created some difficulties for TK. The new board of directors, which were appointed in early 2003, took a lot of measures in order to improve the financial conditions of the company. The company management started to work by determining new strategies to develop new lines and to expand its aircraft fleet.

In June of 2006, the board of directors of TK decided to participate in the Star Alliance, which is a global airline alliance, and its official membership was accepted in 2008. TK incorporated its maintenance department (Turkish Technic), providing its technical maintenances, and made it possible for the company to provide services to the other airlines in the region. In 2006, TK and the catering company Do&Co established the Turkish Do&Co with a 50-50 % partnership, and the catering quality was significantly increased with this cooperation. After the Boeing 777, leased from Jet Airways, began operation, the Turkish Do&Co started their catering service in first-class flights as well at the end of the year 2006. With an agreement made between OPET and TK, the TK OPET Aviation Fuels Inc. was established in order to meet the fuel needs of the aircraft. While TK Technical was continuing its successful maintenance and repair operations, the Turkish Engine Center started to give service after completing its construction activities in Istanbul Sabiha Gökçen Airport with the Pratt & Whitney partnership in order to perform the maintenance of engines.

At a ceremony, an agreement protocol was signed between TK and Star Alliance regarding the participation of TK to Star Alliance. After this development, an intensive work to last 16 months was initiated in the related units of the company in order to meet Star Alliance's participation requirements. This work covered a lot of areas including flight boards at the airports and computer systems to ensure the calculations to be made between airline companies. The first requirement of the Star Alliance agreement is to make agreements about frequent-flier programs (FFP) with 19 airline companies. This process was initiated by conducting the first meetings with Lufthansa at the beginning of 2007. FFP cooperation between Lufthansa and TK was launched on 1 April 2007. TK participated in Star Alliance at a ceremony held on 1 April 2008 (THY 2999).

FFP agreements with other airlines were also entered into force on that date. In addition to the FFP agreements with the member airlines, special prorate agreements and code-share agreements were also initiated quickly. Today while Turkish Airlines has over 100 direct flight destinations abroad, it has achieved an opportunity to fly its passengers to more than 1000 destinations with the Star Alliance cooperation. While TK was expanding its flight network, it also continued to work toward becoming a well-known brand all around the world by being a member of Star Alliance. After private companies entered the market, TK was forced to compete in prices, and as a result, it launched a low-rate airline service, with the AnadoluJet sub-brand based in Ankara on 23 April 2008. The airplane crash that occurred during landing in Amsterdam Airport on 25 February 2009 caused the revision of all flight-related processes. With the agreement made between TK and Havaş, a subsidiary company of TAV, on 1 January 2010, Turkish Ground Services (TGS) was established in order to give ground operation service in airports. Upon inspection of AU service quality by the international audit firm, Skytrax, AU was promoted to four-star airline category at the end of 2007 (Gökırmak 2014).

5.4 SWOT Analysis

SWOT is defined as a situation analysis for any foundations', destinations', or products' strengths, weaknesses, opportunities, and threats analysis. It helps to focus on strengths to minimize weakness and to take the greatest possible advantage of opportunities available (Pahl and Richter 2009). Opportunities are elements of external environment which provide advantages to foundations about a specific target or group of targets, while threats on the contrary are any environmental developments which provide problems for foundations. Strengths, on the other hand, represent the distinguished and specific characteristics of foundations; conversely, weaknesses are the preventing and limiting characteristics of foundations.

TK's competitive position in the international aviation industry and brand management is researched in this study. Skytrax criteria of the year 2013, which star airline companies from one star to five stars, were used for SWOT analysis. To compare TK's strengths and weaknesses, SQ was chosen since the airline is getting five stars from Skytrax almost every year and it is undoubtedly the most consistent Skytrax's five-starred airline. "Web site and general rating," "business class products and service ratings," and "economy class products and service ratings" of both TK and SQ airlines are demonstrated in Tables 5.2, 5.3, and 5.4. TK is not in the lead of any criteria which could be the most impressive result of all three tables. On the other hand, apart from the equal ones, SQ is half star in the lead in some criteria, one star in some criteria, and one and a half star in the lead of some other criteria. These differences are shown on the tables as "*" (minimum) for half star, "**" (medium) for one star, and "***" (maximum) for one and a half star.

Strengths, weaknesses, opportunities, and threats were summarized in Table 5.4. The criteria mentioned in Tables 5.2, 5.3, and 5.4 were simply moved to Table 5.5 as strengths and weaknesses under three topic titles: *Web site and general rating, business class product and service rating, and economy class product and service rating.* Opportunities and threats on the other hand were summarized, taking the differences on strengths and weaknesses into consideration.

As can be seen in Table 5.5, receiving five stars from Skytrax is not far away from TK when especially "threats" are considered. Although "cleanliness" seems to

Table 5.1 Evaluation criteria for Taiwan Airlines

Category of criteria	Evaluation criteria
Onboard comfort	Cleanness and onboard noise level
	Onboard facilities such as seat comfort and width
	Onboard services including catering and newspapers
Personnel	Helpful attitude and kindness of check-in staff
	Stewardesses' concern
	Appearance and kindness of the airline staff
	Efficiency of the airline staff
Service reliability	Accidents related to safety
	Safety and security measures of the airline
	On-time performance
	Frequency of service and convenience of schedules
Convenience of service	Convenience of services before and after the flight
Handling of abnormal conditions	Handling customer complaints or underperformance
	Handling flight delays
	Handling lost baggage or damage

Table 5.2 Web sites and general ratings of TK and SQ

Web site and general rating	TK (Star)	SQ (Star)
Web site : ease of use	4	4
Web site: product information	4	4
Web site: online check-in	4	4
*Staff grooming and presentation**	*3.5*	*4*
*Handling delays/cancelations***	*4*	*5*
Age of aircraft in fleet	4	4
Cabin safety standards	4	4
*Cockpit communications***	*3*	*4*
Airline onboard magazine	4	4
Assisting families and children	4	4

*Minimum difference; **medium difference

be the most important difference (***) from the table, and therefore the first threat, "delays and cancelations" (**) threat is undoubtedly a prior problem and topic to handle since the other threats could be solved easier.

5.5 Conclusion

Globalization effect pushed many companies – even multinational companies – to accept the world as one market and go for one global market with one global brand. The aviation industry and airline companies are not exceptions to this phenomenon.

Table 5.3 Business class products and service ratings of TK and SQ

Business class product and service rating	TK (Star)	SQ (Star)
Airport services		
Check-in services	4	4
*Transfer services***	*3*	*4*
*Priority boarding***	*3*	*4*
*Arrival assistance**	*3.5*	*4*
Arrival lounges	N/A	N/A
*Baggage delivery**	*4*	*4.5*
Business class lounge		
*Lounge comfort, space***	*4*	*5*
Washroom, shower facilities	4	4
Dining options/food quality	4.5	4.5
*Internet/WiFi options***	*4*	*5*
Staff: service efficiency	4	4
*Staff: enthusiasm, attitude**	*3.5*	*4*
Staff: problem solving	4	4
Staff: language skills	4	4
Long-haul flights		
Onboard product		
Seat comfort	4.5	4.5
*Comfort: blankets, pillows***	*4*	*5*
*In-flight entertainment***	*4*	*5*
*Washroom cleanliness****	*3.5*	*5*
*Cabin cleanliness and condition**	*4*	*4.5*
Quality of meals served	4	4
*Dine-on-demand efficiency****	*3*	*4.5*
*Newspapers and magazines***	*4*	*5*
Cabin staff service		
*Service efficiency**	*4*	*4.5*
*Enthusiasm, attitude**	*3.5*	*4*
*Interaction with PAX***	*3.5*	*4.5*
*Cabin presence thru flight***	*4*	*5*
*Responding to requests**	*3.5*	*4*
*Language skills***	*4*	*5*
Consistency among staff	4	4
Regional flights		
Onboard product		
Seat comfort	4	4
Comfort: blankets, pillows	4	4
In-flight entertainment	4	4
*Washroom cleanliness***	*4*	*5*
Quality of meals served	4	4

(continued)

Table 5.3 (continued)

Business class product and service rating	TK (Star)	SQ (Star)
*Cabin cleanliness and condition**	*4*	*4.5*
*Newspapers and magazines****	*3.5*	*5*
Cabin staff service		
*Service efficiency***	*4*	*5*
Enthusiasm, attitude	4	4
*Interaction with PAX**	*3.5*	*4*
*Cabin presence thru flight***	*4*	*5*
*Responding to requests**	*4*	*4.5*
*Language skills**	*3.5*	*4*
Friendliness and hospitality	4	4

*Minimum difference; **medium difference; ***maximum difference

Table 5.4 Economy class products and service ratings of TK and SQ

Economy class product and service rating	TK (Star)	SQ (Star)
Airport services		
Check-in services	4	4
*Transfer services***	*3*	*4*
*Arrival assistance***	*3*	*4*
Baggage delivery	4	4
Long-haul flights		
Onboard product		
Seat comfort	4	4
Comfort: blankets, pillows	4	4
*In-flight entertainment***	*4*	*5*
*Washroom cleanliness****	*3*	*4.5*
*Cabin cleanliness and condition***	*4*	*5*
Quality of meals served	4	4
Quantity of food served	4	4
*Newspapers and magazines***	*3*	*4*
Cabin staff service		
*Service efficiency***	*4*	*5*
*Enthusiasm, attitude**	*4*	*4.5*
*Interaction with PAX***	*3*	*4*
*Cabin presence thru flight**	*4*	*4.5*
*Responding to requests**	*4*	*4.5*
*Language skills**	*3.5*	*4*
*Consistency among staff***	*3.5*	*4.5*
Friendliness and hospitality	4	4
Regional flights		

(continued)

Table 5.4 (continued)

Economy class product and service rating	TK (Star)	SQ (Star)
Onboard product		
Seat comfort	4	4
*Comfort: blankets, pillows**	*3.5*	*4*
In-flight entertainment	4	4
Washroom cleanliness	4	4
*Cabin cleanliness and condition**	*4*	*4.5*
Quality of meals served	4	4
Quantity of food served	4	4
Cabin staff service		
*Service efficiency***	*4*	*5*
Enthusiasm, attitude	4	4
*Interaction with PAX**	*3*	*3.5*
*Cabin presence thru flight**	*4*	*4.5*
*Friendliness and hospitality***	*4*	*5*
Language skills	4	4
Responding to requests	4	4

*Minimum difference; **medium difference; ***maximum difference

Table 5.5 Strengths, weakness, opportunities, and threats for TK based on Skytrax criteria

Strengths	Weaknesses
1. Web site and general rating	*1. Web site and general rating*
Web site: ease of use	Cockpit communications**
Web site: product information	Handling delays/cancelations**
Web site: online check-in	Staff grooming and presentation*
Age of aircraft in fleet	
Airline onboard magazine	
Assisting families and children	
2. Business class product and service rating	*2. Business class product and service rating*
Airport services	*Airport services*
Check-in services	Transfer services**
Business class lounge	Priority boarding**
Washroom, shower facilities	Arrival assistance*
Dining options/food quality	Baggage delivery*
Staff: service efficiency	*Business class lounge*
Staff: problem solving	Lounge comfort, space**
Staff: language skills	Internet/WiFi options**
	Staff: enthusiasm, attitude*

(continued)

Table 5.5 (continued)

Strengths	Weaknesses
Long-haul flights	*Long-haul flights*
Seat comfort	Washroom cleanliness***
Quality of meals served	Dine-on-demand efficiency***
	Comfort: blankets, pillows**
	In-flight entertainment**
	Newspapers and magazines**
	Cabin cleanliness and condition*
Long-haul flights cabin staff service	*Long-haul flights* cabin staff service
Consistency among staff	Interaction with PAX**
	Cabin presence thru flight**
	Language skills**
	Service efficiency*
	Enthusiasm, attitude*
	Responding to requests*
Regional flights	*Regional flights*
Seat comfort	Newspapers and magazines***
Comfort: blankets, pillows	Washroom cleanliness**
In-flight entertainment	Cabin cleanliness and condition*
Quality of meals served	
Regional flights cabin staff service	*Regional flights cabin staff service*
Friendliness and hospitality	Service efficiency**
Enthusiasm, attitude	Cabin presence thru flight**
	Interaction with PAX*
	Responding to requests*
	Language skills*
3. *Economy class product and service rating*	3. *Economy class product and service rating*
Airport services	*Airport services*
Check-in services	Transfer services**
Baggage delivery	Arrival assistance**
Long-haul flights	*Long-haul flights*
Seat comfort	Washroom cleanliness***
Comfort: blankets, pillows	In-flight entertainment**
Quality of meals served	Cabin cleanliness and condition**
Quantity of food served	Newspapers and magazines**
Long-haul flights cabin staff service	*Long-haul flights* cabin staff service
Friendliness and hospitality	Service efficiency**
	Interaction with PAX**
	Consistency among staff**
	Enthusiasm, attitude*
	Cabin presence thru flight*
	Responding to requests*
	Language skills*

(continued)

Table 5.5 (continued)

Strengths	Weaknesses
Regional flights	*Regional flights*
Seat comfort	Comfort: blankets, pillows*
In-flight entertainment	Cabin cleanliness and condition*
Washroom cleanliness	
Quality of meals served	
Quantity of food served	
Regional flights cabin staff service	*Regional flights cabin staff service*
Enthusiasm, attitude	*Service efficiency***
	*Friendliness and hospitality***
	*Interaction with PAX**
Language skills	*Cabin presence thru flight**
Responding to requests	
Opportunities	Threats
Emirates' "ice TV" (i for information, c for communication, and e for entertainment) is already a brand for in-flight entertainment. TK could name the system to obtain a brand image	Washroom and cabin cleanliness
The good image on TK's meal quality could turn out to "TK's meal is the best" with supporting instruments	Efficient responses to food and beverage requirements
Several languages spoken flights are popular on top-rated airlines. TK could employ foreigner cabin staffs either for global brand for employees or having a staff speaking many languages in flights.	The week variety of newspapers and magazines offered
	The look, communication style, and presentation of cabin staff
	Delays and cancelations
	Transfers and arrival assistance

*Minimum difference; **medium difference; ***maximum difference

The airline companies have been trying to be global brands in the progress by either acquiring smaller corporations or entering new destinations to extend market share or taking the advantages of their home countries' geographical positions.

Turkish flag carrier TK is becoming a global airline brand by taking advantage of Turkey's geographical position – connecting Europe, Asia and the Middle East – and adding new connecting flights (more than 200 flight destinations as the airline announced on their official Web site). Moreover, TK has invested firstly on the quality of meal and its service (flying chefs) in order to build a strong brand image on service quality and product differentiation fields.

Today, TK is unquestionably one of the brightest stars in the Eurasia region, enjoying profitable growth, receiving Europe's best airline award for the last 4 years (including 2014), improving in the list of "world's Top 10 Airlines" (fifth in 2014), and compelling expansion opportunities. However, the airline is still four starred by Skytrax criteria, and "five star" is such a privilege and brand image for the airline industry.

Taking SQ as benchmark and BIC, the strengths and weaknesses of TK in the global branding process as well as opportunities and threats were investigated in this study. The results revealed that TK has significant weaknesses on three main topics which are "cleanliness," "staff presentation," and "handling delays/cancelations."

This particular study is not without limitations. SWOT analysis itself is being argued nowadays with its intrinsic nature. Consumers are not represented with the single level of analysis. In summary, there are other fundamental concerns about SWOT analysis (Hill and Westbrook 1997):

- The length of the lists.
- No requirement to prioritize or weight the factors identified.
- Unclear and ambiguous words and phrases.
- No resolution of conflicts (as with the example given in the preceding paragraph).
- No obligation to verify statements and opinions with data or analyses.
- Single level of analysis is all that is required.
- No logical link with an implementation phase.

Furthermore, the SWOT instruments used in this study were not acquired from the consultants but from the consumer evaluations of Skytrax. Taking all these limitations into consideration, future consumer and/or consultant perception studies with other statistical analysis comparing airlines' performances would contribute in the literature.

References

Air Transport Association of America (2007) The airline handbook, Chapter 4. http://airlines.org/ATAResources/Handbook/Pages/AirlineHandbookChapter4AirlineEconomics.aspx

Aircraft Aerodynamics and Design Group Stanford University (2011). "The airline industry" http://adg.stanford.edu/aa241/intro/airlineindustry.html

Alkoç H (2004) Havayolu İşletmelerinin Hizmet Kalitesi Açısından Değerlendirilmesi Üzerine Bir Pilot Araştırma: Türk Hava Yolları Uygulaması. İstanbul Üniversitesi Sosyal Bilimler Enstitüsü. Yüksek Lisans Tezi, Istanbul

Betts P (1994) A slow flight back into profit-the pain for airlines is by no means over. Financial Times, 2. September 1994

Brymer C (2009) The nature of marketing. Macmillan, Palgrave

Caldwell N, Freire JR (2004) The differences between branding a country, a region and a city: applying the brand box model. J Brand Manag 12(1):50–61

Cass A, Ngo L (2007) Market orientation versus innovative culture: two routes to superior brand performance. Eur J Market 41(7/8):868–888

Çelik D (2012) Havayolu İşletmelerinde Performans Yönetimi ve Dengeli Sonuç Kartı: Havayolu İşletmelerinde Bir Araştırma. Unpublished thesis, Anadolu Üniversitesi Sosyal Bilimler Enstitüsü, Eskişehir

Chang Y-H, Yeh C-H (2002) A survey analysis of service quality for domestic airlines. Eur J Oper Res 139:166–171

Chinomona R, Mahlangu D, Pooe D (2003) Brand service quality, satisfaction, trust and preference as predictors of consumer brand loyalty in the retailing industry. Med J Soc Sci 4(14):181–190
Clemes MD, Gan C, Kao TH, Choong M (2008) An empirical analysis of customer satisfaction in international air travel. Innov Market 4(2):49–62
Cop R, Bekmezci M (2005) Marka ve Bilinirliliği Yüksek Markalı Çamasır Deterjanı Üzerine Bir Uygulama. Ticaret ve Turizm Eğitim Fakültesi Dergisi 1:66–81
Driver CJ (1999) Developments in airline marketing practice. J Market Pract Appl Market Sci 5(5):134–150
Elitok B (2003) Hadi Markalaşalım. Sistem Yayıncılık, İstanbul
Elliot KM, Roach DW (1993) Service quality in the airline industry: are carriers getting an unbiased evaluation from consumers? J Prof Serv Mark 9:71–82
Erturk M (2011) İşletme Biliminin Temel İlkeleri. Beta Basım A.Ş, Istanbul
Gökırmak H (2014) Türk Hava Yolları'nın Havacılık Sektöründekı Konumu. Siyaset, Ekonomi ve Yönetim Araştırmaları Dergisi 2(2/4):1–29
Gremler DD, Brown SW (1996) Service loyalty: its nature, importance, and implications. In: Edvardsson B, Brown SW, Johnston R et al (eds) Advancing service quality: a global perspective. International Service Quality Association, pp 171–180
Grönroos C (1984) A service quality model and its marketing implications. Eur J Market 18(4):36–44; Parasuraman A, Zeithaml VA, Berry LL (1985) A conceptual model of services quality and its implication for future research. J Market 49(4):41–50
Grönroos C (2007) Service management and marketing. Customer management in service competition. Wiley, Chichester
Harris LC, Goode MMH (2004) The four levels of loyalty and the pivotal role of trust: a study of online service dynamics. J Retail 80(2):139–158
Hill T, Westbrook R (1997) SWOT analysis: it's time for a product recall. Long Range Plann 30(1):46–52
Kolb BM (2006) Tourism marketing for cities & towns: using branding & events to attract tourists. Routledge, New York
Kotler P (2001) Kotler on marketing. Free Press, New York
Liou JJH, Tzeng G-H (2007) A non-additive model for evaluating airline service quality. J Air Transp Manag 13(3):131–138
Liou JH, Tang CH, Yeh WC, Tsai CY (2011) A decision rules approach for improvement of airport service quality. Expert Syst Appl 38:13723–13730
Morton J (1994) Predicating brand preference. J Market Manag 2(4):32–44
Okumuş A, Asil H (2007) Hizmet Kalitesi Algılamasını Havayolu Yolcularının Genel Memnuniyet Düzeylerine Olan Etkisinin İncelenmesi. İstanbul Üniversitesi İşletme Fakültesi İşletme Dergisi 36(2):10–13
Onan G (2006) Hizmet sektöründe marka sadakati ve TEB üzerine bir uygulama. Unpublished thesis, Dokuz Eylül Üniversitesi Sosyal Bilimler Enstitüsü
Ostrowski RL, O'Brien TV, Gordon GL (1993) Service quality and customer loyalty in the commercial airline industry. J Travel Res 32(2):16–24
Pahl N, Richter A (2009) SWOT analysis. Idea, methodology and a practical approach. GRIN Verlag GmbH
Parasuraman A, Zeithaml VA, Berry LL (1985) A conceptual model of service quality and its implications for future research. J Mar Sci 49:41–50
Parasuraman A, Zeithaml VA, Berry LL (1988) SERVQUAL: multiple-item scale for measuring consumer perceptions of service quality. J Retail 64(1):12–40
Parasuraman A, Zeithaml V, Berry LL (1994) Reassessment of expectations as a comparison standard in measuring service quality: implications for future research. J Mar Sci 58:111–124
Sezgin E (2008) Brand image management: perceptions of European tour operators in single tourism market concept. Tourism 56(2):173–183

Sezgin E, Kozak R (2012) Surviving in the airline business with a brand image; perception of travel agency ticketing employees on Turkish airlines. Int J Bus Soc Sci 3(12):290–296
Sivadas E, Baker-Prewitt JL (2000) An examination of the relationship between service quality, customer satisfaction, and store loyalty. J Retail Distrib Manag 28(2):73–82
Skapinker M (1995) Airbus and Boeing decide big may not be that beautiful. Financial Times, 14 July 1995.
Tam JLM (2013) The effects of service quality, perceived value and customer satisfaction on behavioral intentions. J Hospit Leisure Market 6(4):31–44
Taneja NK (2003) Airline survival kit. Ashgate, Aldershot
Taneja NK (2014) Designing future-oriented airline businesses. Ashgate, Burlington, pp 110
THY, http://investor.turkishairlines.com/tr/thy-anonim-ortakligi/tarihce
Turkish Airlines gears up to enhance market share, October 15, 2008. Accessed at: http://www.expresstravelworld.com/20081015/edge02.shtml
Turkish Airlines orders Mechtronix Ascent XJ Trainer, 20 February 2010. Accessed at: http://www.mechtronix.com/c/mech/file_db/News_Pdf_e/Turkishairlinesfinal_110708_EN.pdf
Why's Turkish the atypical Middle Eastern airline brand? January 22, 2010. Accessed at: http://bx.businessweek.com/airline-industry/view?url=http%3A%2F%2Fsimpliflying.com%2F2009%2Fturkish-airlines-the-atypical-middle-eastern-airline-brand-ceo-dr-temel-kotil-outlines-global-dreams-in-interview%2F
www.marketingpower.com
Zeithaml VA, Parasuraman A, Berry LL (1985) Problems and strategies in services marketing. J Market 49(2):33–46, Spring 1985
Zeithaml VA, Berry LL, Parasuraman A (1993) The nature and determinants of customer expectations of service. J Acad Market Sci 21(1):1–12
Zeithaml VA, Berry LL, Parasuraman A (1996) The behavioral consequences of service quality. J Market 60(2):31–46

Erkan Sezgin He graduated and received his Ph.D. in tourism management from Anadolu University. Erkan Sezgin has improved with specialization in information communication technology applications in tourism, as well as travel business and airline industry. His research area – namely, articles and conference papers – consists of corporate branding and information technologies of mainly travel companies and airline companies. He is currently Deputy Dean of Tourism Faculty at Anadolu University.

Deniz Yuncu She graduated and received her Ph.D. in tourism management in Anadolu University. She has two major streams of research interest. The first is in consumer behavior, event, and destination marketing. The second stream of research is marketing researches including social network analysis and qualitative research methods in tourism. She is currently Assistant Professor of Tourism Faculty at Anadolu University.

Chapter 6
Managing Development of Resort Destinations in Southeast Asia: Emerging and Peripheral Phu Quoc Island

Vo Phuoc Quang Pham and K. Thirumaran

Abstract Southeast Asia located in the tropics offers a variety of sea resort destinations. With the recent economic reforms in Vietnam, Cambodia, and Myanmar for greater integration into the world economy, tourism has been a key sector of attention with many potential sea resorts to be developed in these countries' coastal regions. In this regard, Bali and Phuket among others offer important development lessons within the region for Vietnam's rising and popular resort – Phu Quoc Island. This chapter takes a leaf from Bali's tourism experience as a development strategy that can be learned and considered for Phu Quoc Island's growth. Though these destinations are in different stages of development, such comparative learning provides a new perspective on managing peripheral resorts. Utilizing peripheral areas in tourism development theories as a basis to understand Balinese experience, a framework of key factors such as foreign investments and good environmental practices will be examined. Balinese tourism successes and challenges are analyzed to discern ways in which Phu Quoc Island's development can be managed in the twenty-first century as one of several emerging resort destinations in Southeast Asia.

Keywords Sea Resort destinations • Phu Quoc Island • Managing peripheral resorts • New perspective

V.P.Q. Pham (✉)
Tourism and Hospitality and Business Management, James Cook University, Singapore Campus, Townsville City, QLD, Australia
e-mail: quang4404@gmail.com

K. Thirumaran, Ph.D.
JCU, Singapore, Singapore
e-mail: k.thirumaran@jcu.edu.au

P. Mandal, J. Vong (eds.), *Development of Tourism and the Hospitality Industry in Southeast Asia*, Managing the Asian Century,
DOI 10.1007/978-981-287-606-5_6

6.1 Introduction

Destinations like Bali, Indonesia; Phuket, Thailand; Boracay, Philippines; Sentosa, Singapore; and many others around the world offer good pathways of growth for emerging destinations. Of these, Bali is selected to understand some aspects of its growth strategies, which are sufficiently useful for emerging destinations like Phu Quoc to discern and adapt as it emerges from a sleeping domestic resort to a popular international destination in the market reform era in Vietnam.

Bali has been a destination even before the Dutch occupied it in 1905. Its exotic culture attracted many western interests and recognizing its potential, the Suharto regime of independent Indonesia in the 1960s onwards, through a series of plans, built infrastructures to facilitate international carriers and road links to Singaraja, Ubud to Denpasar-Kuta, and nearby districts. Hence, Bali succeeded to be a major tourist destination in Southeast Asia for many international visitors. In recent decades, Bali has been enjoying steady growth in its tourists' arrivals. Bali received 1,412,839 tourists in 2000 (Bali Tourism Board 2014), and latest figures for 2013 shows a record number of 3.27 million tourists (Citrinot 2014). With the threat of terrorism reduced and changing fortunes of global political economy, Bali is poised to hit higher tourists' arrival marks in the future.

Phu Quoc, on the other hand, had been a destination mostly for locals but had not developed much as a key destination internationally. This was mainly due to a shortfall in tourism planning policies prior to market reform initiatives and national socioeconomic priorities. With the dissipation of the Cold War from the mid-1980s onwards, the termination of Vietnam's occupation of Cambodia, membership into ASEAN, with Doi Moi [economic reform policy] introduced, and the recognition of a need for foreign investments and participation in global exchanges, Vietnam automatically became a tourists' destination with many of its heritage and nature-based resources as attractions to be discovered. It is in this latter context that Phu Quoc, among many other attractions in Vietnam, is emerging as a destination. Phu Quoc is 574 km^2, the largest island in Vietnam. Phu Quoc has pristine clean waters and its beaches offer water sports and holidays in the sun with the potential to be the next most popular destination in Southeast Asia. As a tropical island, Phu Quoc enjoys an average temperature of 28 °C, idyllic for beach tourists. About 500,000–600,000 visitors arrive into Phu Quoc Island and of these 40 % are internationals (Thanh Nien News 2014a).

Given the location of both Bali and Phu Quoc in the context of Indonesia and Vietnam respectively, we can state that they are in the peripheral regions and have an important role in the tourism development projects of each country. The issue of land management, development, and degradation of the environment is something that can be learned from Bali's management policies. Utilizing the theory of peripheral areas tourism and conducting a checklist of significant ways Bali had developed as a tourist destination, this chapter seeks to identify key areas Phu Quoc needs to focus as it increasingly becomes an international destination similar to that of Bali, Phuket, and Boracay.

6.2 Literature Review

Periphery destinations are usually vaction areas where people from developed and centers of production travel for their holidays (Muller and Jannson 2006). Geographically, the periphery refers to a place remote to the main sites of activities. Pleasure periphery as used by Turner and Ash (1975) and Christaller (1964) referred to the escape from the urban industrial work cities to places in a distance for relaxation and rejuvenation. As Muller and Jannson (2006) suggest, peripheral areas stand as complimentary development areas for people in the urban centers of Europe. So the development in these areas has to be different and yet managed in a way that present and future generations can enjoy. In Finland and other Nordic countries, tourism in the peripheral regions has increasingly contributed to employment and development (Saarinen 2006).

Islands need not necessarily have a strong state hand in its development. Fischer (2012) writes that Nantucket islanders who had long depended on whale oil exports, in 1888, found their island economy in decline. An unplanned development took place. A recognized Coffins family organized one of the largest reunion of the Coffins with 500 of them descending on Nantucket. Later, the new lodgings built to house the invited Coffins were to serve as a tourist accommodation which Nantucket leveraged and prospered ever since, attracting regular flow of tourists to the island. Other islands such as Germany's Heligoland and Norderney flourished as a result of an upper class and later the middle class seeking retreats such as seaside spa and bathing (Fischer 2012). These and many other highlighted examples reveal that islands, whether they become a successful resort destination, are quite dependent on the vagaries of their economic circumstances and a trigger to create a service economy. In the case of Nantucket in particular, once the infrastructure was in place, it then led to higher visitor arrivals as is corroborated with the novel Moby-Dick by Melville (1851).

In their study of resort development, Botterill et al. (2014) focus on the way in which Caraguatatuba experienced an influx of in-migration creating a stratified class fueling alcohol, drugs, and sex industry in conjunction with rapid resort developments. They argue that development is often depicted in a positive imagery overlaying a veneer of transgressive social pathologies. On the other end of the spectrum, Ioannides (1992) and Pearce (1989) find that in the case of Cypress, the spatial changes and growth are very much shaped by the state actors despite an overwhelming presence of transnational businesses. Hence, depending on the stakeholder's lead, there can be a variety of different outcomes of a destination's development.

Indonesia development planning is based on "center-periphery" as inner and outer zone (Rodenburg 1980). The inner zone includes Bali, Java, and Madura due to their extremely high population densities. Vickers (2011) recounts how Bali's development was very much a narrative of national development from the colonial era to the times when the state of Indonesia was consolidating into a unitary state. In the period of Suharto's reign, significant training institutions along with foreign-managed hotels emerged as Balinese culture, and the beaches became attractions. Many scholarly writings tended to focus on Balinese cultural development more than its beach resorts, precisely because Balinese culture itself was unique and exotic in visitor's eyes differentiated by the many cultures in the Indonesian archipelago.

The literature (Wall 1996; Cohen 1994) also informs us of the existence of a belief system between nature and the Balinese. Due to this established relation, hotel developments and other major developments in Bali have either been thwarted, become controversial, or needed extensive appeasement efforts to overcome the acquisition of land and initiate development. Two examples of projects that were mired in such controversies are a hotel development in close proximity to the sacred Tanah Lot Temple and the towering statue of Wisnu at The Garuda Wisnu Kencana Cultural Park. These controversies partly stem from beliefs that such constructions might upset the spiritual balance of the island of Gods [a synonym for Bali]. As Bell (1992) laments about another challenge that haunts many popular destinations, that is, at times Bali can be also over crowded by tourists and affect the authenticity of cultural performances and the hospitality industry services. Hence, the island paradise as we often come to know is not all devoid of internal challenges.

Thus far, resort development as a topic in Vietnam is scarce. Jansen-Verbeke and Go (1995) and Lam (1996) had earlier on identified the need for the Vietnamese government to take a lead in charting a development path to optimize tourism benefits. Thirumaran et al. (2014) studied the challenges of Vietnam presenting a consolidated brand-souvenir to market the country better. They emphasize the importance of identifying a representative souvenir in an early stage of Vietnam's tourism development. Suntikul et al. (2008) point out the need for different policy bearings on visa, transport, and marketing and ways in which the industry and tourists may be impacted. The authors argue that more liberalization in these three segments is needed to further advance tourism development and arrivals. In these respects, this chapter's examination of Phu Quoc's island further contributes to the literature on Vietnam's tourism development and as a reference for policy makers in view of the challenges that portend as the island's growth is carefully managed in the twenty-first century.

6.3 Methodology

Instead of a direct comparative analysis, this paper presents lessons discerned from an established destination – Bali and attempts to examine an emerging destination – Phu Quoc to understand ways in which the latter can progress as it transforms itself into a major international resort destination. The Vietnamese government in 2012 designated the island as part of coastal economic zone and expected to charter infrastructure developments to the tune of over US$385 million by 2015 (Viet Nam News 2012a). With land use based rentals and extensive road developments, Phu Quoc is well on the way to be a major international tourists' hub. This pattern of development resembles Bali in the 1960s and 1970s, hence a reasonable choice for comparison with Phu Quoc.

Bali is selected to elicit tourism development lessons since the island is one of the most formidable resort destinations in Southeast Asia having survived a series of threats over the years and enjoying an important position in Indonesia's tourism and

MICE hosting center. Bali's success is extensive to the extent that many international, political, economic, and environmental meetings are hosted in Bali, making it almost the second capital after Jakarta. Despite known widely as a popular cultural destination, the island remains a strong attraction for sun seekers and beach surfers coming from mostly Western source markets. It is these beach tourist segments that this chapter explores the lessons appropriate for implementation in Phu Quoc.

Fischer (2012) argues that islands need not develop to the extent that they lose their identity and become the Manhattan or Hong Kong in an attempt to engage in a cosmopolitan life or transform into a purely tourists' island. In this sense, Bali has managed to contain for the most part of tourist activities in designated areas without intruding much into the living space of the ordinary Balinese. Agriculture though has been increasingly displaced by tourism; there is still a degree of continuity in the fisheries and agricultural sector. This is another reason; the island of Gods is selected for Phu Quoc's emulation.

In this reference-comparative study, focusing on lessons that could be learned follows the call by Pearce (1993) to further advance the field to draw out a contrast between two cases. Based mainly on secondary sources such as existing literature and news articles, a number of lessons are drawn on the areas of Bali's tourism development. These areas of interests include infrastructure, hospitality policy or practices, and land-related development issues. A paragon of development model or master plan always runs into multi-sector issues as it does with a variety of socio-cultural links (Prideaux 2009). Thus, as we use Bali as a reference point, Phu Quoc is analyzed contextually within the conditions on the island and Vietnam's national designs to promote tourism.

6.4 Bali: An Indonesian Tourism Project

Bali's policy and planning has been very much from the island's policy makers as well as Jakarta's planning commission. Taking into account the Balinese culture and tourism sector developments, the island had sped fast its time to build world-class resorts and catapulted into a cultural destination. In this section, we examine Bali's growth pattern, zoning scheme, and Balinese industry participation.

In the 1980s, as Bali was enjoying peak tourism arrivals, there were issues related to the way Western beach goers were scantily dressed and making loud merry noises at the bars. At the same time, the Balinese street vendors were also harassing happy beach goers with souvenir sales and massage services. These issues were addressed by the Balinese authorities in an amicable way.

Today, due to the over exploitation of the environment by activities in the tourism industry, Bali is facing a serious environmental degradation issues. One of other issues that also contribute to the harm of environment is the lack of waste management, water scarcity due to the improper water supply, massive land conversion, and increasing traffic jams (Cole 2012). Land-related problems are normally very complex due to the rapid development of tourism industry in Bali. The land scarcity increases the demand of land use for tourism operation and raises conflicting issues

(Rais 1997). The combination of population increase and development activities in both tourism industry and citizen migration has led to competing demands for land.

In the early days of Bali's modern tourism, the government had allocated vast land area to welcome international investors (Vietnam Investment Review 2005). One method in which the Balinese authorities employed was to create designated zones. For example, Nusa Dua is a special zone, most of the hotels matching international standards have been built here exceed in number of rooms than those in the Kuta and outlying regions which have to adhere to a maximum of 40 rooms only. There are many small and medium size hospitality and travel businesses with a small number of individual entrepreneurs since the cost of entry is very low compared to large industry establishment. Indeed, the cost of constructing a room in the early days, 1980, was US$6,218 per room for a small size hotel compared to US$39,444 for a room by international standards (Rodenburg 1980). Most of these small hotels sell rooms directly to their customers. Two-third of the small hotels' customers are independent tourists, the rest are package and group travelers. Due to the enormous amount of investment capacity from international brands and the unfavorable currency exchange rate for operating the business, the large international standard hotels do not generate direct income as much as the small and craft industries do to the Balinese economy and society. More significantly by this practice, Bali has created spaces for small and medium size businesses to flourish alongside the international and recognized brands and established businesses.

6.5 Significant Points of Reference for Phu Quoc

The provincial sea economic development programme for 2011–2015 plan focuses on developing Phu Quoc's ecotourism (Viet Nam News 2012b). In 2004, the government chose Phu Quoc to develop as a center of tourism with regional and international stature. In May 2013, Prime Minister Nguyen Tan Dung decided to cover the whole Phu Quoc Island as a Phu Quoc Special Economic Zone. In October that year, the Ministry of Culture, Sports and Tourism approved the project of planning for sea, island, and coastal tourism development until 2020, including in the project, there is also a plan to build six world-class tourist site destination among Vietnam's coasts, one of them is Phu Quoc. To further boost tourists' arrivals, the Vietnamese government lifted visa requirements for all international travelers with a 30-day stay limit. The only other destination with similar special visa free entry is Da Nang (News VietNamNet 2014). This compares well with Indonesia's policy of granting visa upon arrival for visitors to Bali for some 52 countries. Such international tourist visa arrival policies facilitate expeditious processing of visitor's documentation and encourage higher consideration for the destination.

The government plans reveal 150 development projects. The expected completion of 150 km of roads by 2020 will sufficiently benefit tourists and locals alike. However, according to Van Ha Phong, Chairman of the Phu Quoc District People's

Committee, persuading private investments remains a challenge with the road constructions heavily dependent on government funding (Viet Nam 2012c). The authorities also hoped to develop the island into an international trade center, but a plan would be considered and added to the master plan after the tourism project is completed in 2020. If the idea of an international trade center is implemented, Phu Quoc can also play a major role in attracting MICE (Meetings, Incentives, Conventions and Exhibitions) travelers into Vietnam.

The Phu Quoc People's Committee master plan (Saigoneer 2014) hopes to make the island a center for tourism and commerce. Under the plan, Duong Dong town – the main town of Phu Quoc Island – will be enlarged to a city with 240,000 residents, which is a huge increase from the current 30,000 residents, and will act as a hub for administration, public services, and international commerce. A Thoi also will be enlarged to accommodate 71,000 inhabitants which currently houses around 15,000. The highlight of the new plan is "the sunset corridor" spanning the entire island, connecting major transport hubs, including the airport to the central square, commercial complexes, parks, and tourist markets.

With these developments, Phu Quoc, just like Bali, is not all about tourism and hospitality. Its fishing industry is also receiving attention from the state to further facilitate growth in terms of exports of its seafood production. As part of a future special economic zone, the authorities plan to continue ramping up the development in tourism and primary production industries. Under the master plan for the period of 2004–2010 (Viet Nam News 2013), Phu Quoc has achieved significant socioeconomic development since 2004, the GDP is growing by 22 % annually, and the number of visitors arriving is rapidly increasing. This first master plan has also created special mechanisms and policies for human resource development, immigration, investment, and land management in the new economic zone. The result of which, for example, Vietnam is fully able to mobilize resources to develop and turn Phu Quoc Island into a special economic-administrative hub. The government's exclusive mechanism for Phu Quoc has enabled the highest-ever preferential treatment to have its traffic, infrastructure, and energy systems developed up to its potential.

The Vietnamese effort to develop the island into Southeast Asia's center for tourism, science, and technology extends beyond its shores. Singapore, for example, has signed a cooperation agreement with Vietnam in assisting the latter to implement most favorable investment policies in Phu Quoc. In this respect, Sunray Woodcraft Construction Pte Ltd. and Centurion Properties Pte. Ltd. have allocated 4000 ha of land for ecotourism, urbanization, and hi-tech parks (Thanh Nien News 2014b).

In contrast with other industries that are affected by the world economic crisis, the growth in Vietnam's tourism industry is well and steady due to active promotions from industry players such as hospitality and international aviation services. Phu Quoc in particular can draw lessons from Bali's early tourism development. Similar to Bali, Phu Quoc also holds other attractions beside the spectacular beaches such as pepper farms and tropical agriculture produces that contribute a major percentage to the economy before the rise of tourism. One of these is to promote actively small industries for tourism development among the islanders.

The rapid development of tourism in Phu Quoc also affects the agricultural economy. As tourism becomes more lucrative, young farmers are gradually showing less interest on their farmland and fisheries activities (Wong 1998). The many job opportunities created by tourism have already led to some abandoning their farm cultivation. Phu Quoc has the eco farm with clean vegetable using technology from Israel and produces traditional fish sauce farm for hundred years. It also contains 385 ha of black pepper farmland, and according to government planning policy, it will expand to 500 ha in 2015 and 1000 ha in 2020 (Vietnam Breaking News 2013). This shifting balance is a result of awareness and capitalization of their tropical produce such as the promotion of pepper or local fruit and become an attraction for tourist beside the beach and resort. Here, a dual function for agricultural activities to merge with tourism may contribute to sustainable development in the long term.

Due to the large number of international and nonresident investors with tourism knowledge and capital wherewithal, there is a potential threat that local residents may not be well prepared for this rapid change. Most of the local residents that own land in Phu Quoc's prime area for tourism development are tempted to sell their land for a short-term profit due to the skyrocket land price. Due to this rapid increase in land prices for the last few years, many agriculture farms in Phu Quoc have disappeared. This condition still persists where pepper and other agricultural product's price are in a volatile stage, which in turn might further create an incentive for the farmers to sell their land, and their business may become extinct in the near future. The issue then becomes one of seeking a new economic balance and resource emphasis and allocation.

One of the most critical issues that threaten the development of Phu Quoc is the illegal land acquisition all across the island which has led to the difficulty in proper planning for structural and sustainable accommodation. The island's road network is currently unable to serve mass tourism; however, it is improving as many road constructions are taking place due to the policy changes in Vietnam as Phu Quoc has designated a special economic zone with several targeted development projects assigned. Unclear government policies contribute to potential foreign interests to hesitate investing in this destination, and this can be clarified as one of the biggest barrier. Additionally, local citizens in Phu Quoc have lower educational qualifications compared to urban areas in Vietnam, as there are no tertiary institutions on the island. This has partly also contributed to the unreasonable land prices as many of the citizens are willing to sell their land to investors from Ho Chi Minh City or to foreigners, ignoring advisories from the provincial authorities.

Phu Quoc is being eyed by a dozen of famous luxury hotel chain and resort. For example, Life Resort, a Dutch-Austrian company, and Electricite et Eaux De Madagascar – a French firm and among other foreign investors – are seeking for investment licenses to set up luxury resorts. Saigon Tourist, the leading organization in Vietnam tourism industry, has a plan to build their biggest ecotourism project for an US$85 million that includes 300 hotel rooms and 36-hole golf course. In the course of tourism development and economic sectorial adjustments on the island, the local citizens have quickly adapted and found ways to participate in the tourism industry. Participation accompanied with training programs will empower the younger generation of islanders in Phu Quoc and generate direct income to help them sustain themselves in the new tourism environment.

Under the watchful eyes of the authorities and the people, hotel and beach users including tourists are continuously monitored in Bali to alert sources of pollution to the beaches (The Jakarta Post 2013). Indiscriminate throw of rubbish by hotels and other businesses is often an issue for other beach users (Ni 2011; Bali Post 2014; Desy 2014). In this instance, despite best efforts by various travel organizations, hospitality businesses, governments, and NGOs, the problem remains a stubborn strain on the tourism industry. One of the key activities to preserve Balinese beaches and the nature reserve is the regular cleanup campaign where locals and NGOs participate. Phu Quoc Island being part of the Kien Giang Biosphere Reserve has also come up with a cleanup day campaign (Vietnam News 2012d). Students and residents wore "I Love Phu Quoc" T-shirts to clear litter in the main public areas and tourist sites.

There are many different beach sides on Phu Quoc Island with different levels of exploitation. The beach area near Duong Dong Town has almost reached Bali beach pollution level – by less responsible visitors to the site. Perhaps government policy and planning needs further strengthening and support of protecting this natural resource. Sao Beach site, which is quite far away from Duong Dong town, has very few decent accommodations for tourists. Sao Beach can be a competitive destination site since the beach still contains pure and clean water. However, electricity and water supply are not ready yet for the proper development in accommodation and other services.

6.6 Concluding Remarks

For now, the island of Phu Quoc is ready to accept more international visitors. From November 2014 onwards, Vietnam Airlines has started direct flights to Singapore and Siem Reap. These destinations are the potential market, which have seen an increasing number of tourists come to Phu Quoc year by year (Dinh 2014). Beginning early 2014, Phu Quoc International Airport received Russian tourists with direct flights from Moscow by few different air carriers. Russia is one of the main target markets since Russians appreciate the warm weather in Phu Quoc. As Wong (Wong 1998) correctly identifies the importance of airport links to coastal resorts that are peripheral, Phu Quoc's increased connectivity with domestic airports like Ho Chi Minh and Hanoi and international airports such as Siam Reap (Cambodia) and Singapore makes sense for its immediate development. The peak period is between October and December when Russians travel to avoid the cold harsh weather in their homeland. A combination of visa-free immigration process, international flight connections, accommodations, and infrastructure have been steadily put in place and aligned to receive more tourists. In this sense, Phu Quoc in the z century is poised to be a leading holiday destination that may follow other more mature destinations like Bali, Phuket, and Boracay. Phu Quoc's development is timely. When the ASEAN Economic Community (AEC) comes into effect in Dec 2015, Phu Quoc would be ready to receive even larger number of tourists with its current infrastructure steadily put in place.

The role of Phu Quoc in Vietnam's overall tourism economy is important and what it needs are strategies of development and proper plans. The management and success of resort destination stands as a paradigm in what may happen to other sites along Vietnam's long coastal regions and islands in the south. There is a perception that tourists visiting Southeast Asia are familiar with the more popular destinations of Boracay in the Philippines, Bali in Indonesia, Phuket in Thailand, and several more in the region. A perspective exists that views tourists as seeking new places for different or similar experiences (Thirumaran 2009). In this context, Phu Quoc is emerging as an added resort destination in ASEAN. While currently, Phu Quoc does not distinguish itself from the other resort destinations, the Vietnamese authority can also consider the model of Bali where sea sports facilities are available and Phuket where sea sports are increasingly made into events and competitions thus enhancing the destination's viability further. By Based on the master plans, all indications suggest, Phu Quoc heading in the direction of a MICE destination.

Bali's sustainable tourism is a continuous project among different institutions involving local and international organizations (Wall 1992; Bater 2000; Macrory 2013). These efforts take into account ways Balinese culture remains intact with implementation of sustainable practices to protect the natural environment from the impact of tourism. While the Balinese people have a religious-social link to land and nature that creates a space for negotiating current or future developments despite the often top-down approach, Phu Quoc Island on the other hand is containing its development in carefully studied plans and implementation program.

One crucial question remains, if developing a resort in a region that is already filled with similar articulations, will Phu Quoc emerge as a competitor? Other regions in Vietnam too such as Danang appear to offer good seaside vacation as much as the continuing attractiveness of the Pacific Islands. Perhaps diversification within the resort development context could be the way forward. We now know that the Vietnamese authorities are in full throttle of key developments essential for facilitating tourism, one of which is a passenger port (World Market Intelligence News 2014; Asia News Monitor 2014). In 2005, the Vietnam Investment Review revealed plans of Victoria Hotels and Resorts group to invest in resorts at the cost of US$12 million in which it was also pointed out that "Developers believe the island could eventually become another Bali." Since then many more international hospitality firms have invested in setting up hotels and restaurants and combined with airport connections, Phu Quoc's success can be measured in terms of success on the foreign direct investments and inflow of tourists as well as opportunities for locals to further engage in the service economy of tourism.

Managing sea front resorts is not an easy or a short-term task. The project involves careful planning and timely or periodic interventions by the state to govern allocation of space, resources, and creation of activities aligned with preservation of the environment to benefit the people living in close proximity to that destination.

The extent state intervention limits negative environmental impacts (Bramwell 2004) is as crucial as efforts made by the private sector and signification to tourists' behaviors. In the tourism development history of a country, sometimes investments can pour in to already established destinations, while it may take years before peripheral areas receive similar attention for development (Grumo and Ivona 2005) or be part of a larger marketing strategy. Hence, Hall's (2000) "boosterism" strategy is necessary if the state were to take Phu Quoc to its ideal finality, an island resort destination. Wong's (1998) study of tourism in coastal regions of Southeast Asia offers lessons of managing developments. The importance of environmental impact study, managing tourist capacity, integrating tourism development into local economies and mindful of conservation of heritage and natural resources. Of these, Phuo Quoc is well placed to learn from other unplanned resorts like Pattaya and Patong Beach in Thailand as well as Kuta in Bali during the initial phases.

While this chapter examines the development aspects of Phu Quoc, a few important issues have yet to be distilled. These issues relate primarily to marketing and the tourism frame in which Phu Quoc would be thrusted into the region where island vacations are abundant. Bali had promoted itself as the Island of Paradise with an emphasis on culture within Indonesia's larger push to promote itself as a cultural destination. It is observable from the many international meetings and high number of surfboarders attracted to Bali that aside from infrastructure building, success also emanates from Indonesia-Bali marketing efforts. Phuket on the other hand has increasingly emphasized water sports events. Taking marine tourism a step further, the new military regime in Bangkok has revealed a plan to brand Phuket as the "Riviera of Asia" to further promote cruise ship arrivals. The authorities concerned with Phu Quoc's development plan have to go further in deciding the type of resort destination the island would eventually be in a region dotted with the familiar.

References

Asia News Monitor (2014) Vietnam: Hundreds projects given go-ahead on phu quoc island. http://search.proquest.com/docview/1476522459?accountid=16285. Accessed 11 Jan 2015

Bali Post (2014) Jelang MEA, Sampah Jadi Ancaman Pariwisata Bali. https://docs.google.com/document/d/1afTHMosC7_eN3_myPNcC8Koj364IvJqgbXaSyNKIDLE/edit#. Accessed 15 Nov 2014

Bali Tourism Board (2014) Direct foreign arrivals to Bali by market country 2000–2005. http://www.balitourismboard.org/files/By%20Region%202000-2005.pdf. Accessed 10 Nov 2014

Bater JH (2000) Capacity building for environmental management in Indonesia: lessons from the Bali sustainable development project. J Transnat Manag Dev 4(3–4):107–134

Bell CA (1992) Bali: how to maintain a fragile resort. Cornell Hotel Restaur Admin Q 33(5):28

Botterill D, Seixas SRDC, Hoeffel JL (2014) Tourism and transgression: resort development, crime and the drug economy. Tour Plan Dev 11(1)

Bramwell B (2004) The policy context for tourism and sustainability in Southern Europe's coastal regions. In: Bramwell B (ed) Coastal mass tourism: diversification and sustainable development in Southern Europe. Channel View Publications, Clevedon, pp 32–47

Christaller W (1964) Some considerations of tourism location in Europe: the peripheral regions – underdeveloped countries – recreation areas. Pap Reg Sci 12(1):95–105

Citrinot, Luc (2014) New tourism record for Bali in 2013. http://www.traveldailynews.asia/news/article/55315/new-tourism-record-for-bali. Accessed 19 Jan 2015
Cohen M (1994) God and mammon: luxury resort triggers outcry over Bali's future. Far East Econ Rev 26:28–33
Cole S (2012) A political ecology of water equity and tourism: a case study from Bali. Ann Tour Res 39(2):1221–1241
Desy N (2014) Surf spots polluted with waste. The Jakarta Post. http://www.thejakartapost.com/news/2014/02/13/surf-spots-polluted-with-waste.html. Accessed 15 Nov 2014
Dinh Q (2014) Vietnam airlines opens air services from Phu Quoc to Singapore, Siem Reap. Thanh Nien News. http://www.thanhniennews.com/travel/vietnam-airlines-opens-airservices-from-phu-quoc-to-singapore-siem-reap-31639.html. Accessed 5 Nov 2014
Fischer SR (2012) Islands: From Atlantis to Zanzibar. Reaktion Books, Chicago/London
Grumo R, Ivona A (2005) Tourism in peripheral regions – discovering the hidden histories of Italy. In: Marina Novelli (ed) Niche Tourism. Taylor & Francis, Hoboken, pp 121–131
Hall CM (2000) Tourism planning: policies, processes and relationships. Prentice Hall, New York
Ioannides D (1992) Tourism development agents: The Cypriot resort cycle. Ann Tour Res 19(4):711–731
Jakarta Post (2013) Issues of the day: Bali becomes unattractive to Europeans. http://www.thejakartapost.com/news/2013/03/19/issues-day-bali-becomes-unattractive-europeans.html. Accessed 9 Nov 2014
Jansen-Verbeke M, Go F (1995) Tourism development in Vietnam. Tour Manag 6(14):315–321
Lam CMT (1996) Hotel and tourism development in Vietnam. J Travel Tour Mark 7(1):85–91
Macrory B (2013) Green school in Bali. Green Teach 99:25–27
Melville H (1851) Moby-Dick. Richard Bentley, London
Muller D, Jannson B (2006) The difficult business of making pleasure peripheries prosperous: perspectives on place, space and environment. In Dieter K Muller, B Jansson (eds) Tourism in peripheries: perspectives from the far north and south. CABI, Oxfordshire, pp 3–18
News VietNamNet (2014) Advantages for PhuQuoc island to take off. http://english.vietnamnet.vn/fms/business/96650/advantages-for-phu-quoc-island-to-take-off.html. Accessed 1 Nov 2014
Ni Komang E (2011) Bali hotels, restaurants warned about pollution. The Jakarta Post. http://www.thejakartapost.com/news/2011/08/06/bali-hotels-restaurants-warned-aboutpollution.html. Accessed 9 Nov 2014
Pearce DG (1989) Tourist development. Longman, New York
Pearce DG (1993) Comparative studies in tourism research. In: Pearce DG, Butler RW (eds) Tourism research: critiques and challenges. Routledge, London, pp 20–35
Prideaux B (2009) Resort destinations: evolution, management and development. Routledge, Florence/New York
Rais J (1997) Planning sustainable land management at regional level: the Indonesian case. ITC, pp 273–278. http://wgbis.ces.iisc.ernet.in/energy/HC270799/LM/SUSLUP/KeySpeakers/ARais.pdf. Accessed 15 Nov 2014
Rodenburg E (1980) The effects of scale in economic development: Tourism in Bali. Ann Tour Res 2:177
Saarinen J (2006) Tourism in peripheries: the role of tourism in regional development in Northern Finland. In: Muller DK, Jansson B (eds) Tourism in peripheries: perspectives from the far north and south. CABI, Oxfordshire, pp 41–52
Saigoneer (2014) 2030 Phu Quoc Master Plan Approved. http://saigoneer.com/saigon-development/2344-photos-2030-phu-quoc-master-plan-approved. Accessed 20 Jan 2015
Suntikul W, Butler R, Alrey D (2008) Changing accessibility to Vietnam: the influence of a government in transition. In: Cochrane J (ed) Asian tourism: growth and change. Elsevier, London, pp 69–78
Thanh Nien News (2014a) Tourists not yet enchanted by Vietnam's tourism haven Phu Quoc. http://www.thanhniennews.com/society/tourists-not-yet-enchanted-by-vietnams-tourismhaven-phu-quoc-24633.html. Accessed 13 Nov 2014

Thanh Nien News (2014b) Vietnam taps Singapore to develop Phu Quoc Island. http://www.thanhniennews.com/business/vietnam-taps-singapore-to-develop-phu-quoc-island-25877.html. Accessed 20 Jan 2015

Thirumaran K, Minh DX, Thirumaran CM (2014) Integrating souvenirs with tourism development: Vietnam's challenges. Tour Plan Dev 11(1):57–67

Thirumaran K (2009) Renewing bonds in an age of Asian travel: Indian tourists in Bali. In: Tim Winter, Peggy Teo, T. C. Chang (eds) Asia on tour: exploring the rise of Asian tourism. Taylor & Francis, Abingdon, pp 127–137

Turner L, Ash J (1975) The golden hordes: international tourism and the pleasure periphery. Constable, London

Vickers A (2011) Bali rebuilds its tourist industry. Bijdragen tot de Taal-, Land- en Volkenkunde 167(4):459–481

Viet Nam News (2012a) Plan to update island infrastructure. http://vietnamnews.vn/economy/232261/plan-to-update-island-infrastructure.html. Accessed 2 Nov 2014

Viet Nam News (2012b) Phu Quoc development plan focuses on eco-tourism sector. Viet Nam News. http://vietnamnews.vn/industries/223521/phu-quoc-development-plan-focuseson-eco-tourism-sector.html. Accessed 6 Nov 2014

Viet Nam News (2012c) Phu Quoc development plan focuses on eco-tourism sector. http://vietnamnews.vn/industries/223521/phu-quoc-development-plan-focuses-on-eco-tourism-sector.html. Accessed 15 Jan 2015

Viet Nam News (2012d) Friends of Phu Quoc clean up their island. http://vietnamnews.vn/environment/234003/friends-of-phu-quoc-clean-up-their-island.html. Accessed 16 Jan 2015

Vietnam Breaking News (2013) Phu Quoc Island promotes black pepper. http://www.vietnambreakingnews.com/2013/06/phu-quoc-island-promotes-black-pepper/. Accessed 11 Nov 2014

Vietnam Investment Review (2005) Fantasy island: $12m resort for phu quoc?. http://search.proquest.com/docview/201577125?accountid=16285. Accessed 11 Jan 2015

Vietnam News (2013) High hopes for Phu Quoc's future. http://vietnamnews.vn/economy/244967/high-hopes-for-phu-quocs-future.html. Accessed 20 Jan 2015

Wall G (1996) Perspectives on tourism in selected Balinese villages. Ann Tour Res 23(1):123–137

Wall G (1992) Bali sustainable development project. Ann Tour Res 19(3):569–571

Wong PP (1998) Coastal tourism development in Southeast Asia. Ocean Coast Manag 38(2):89–109

World Market Intelligence News (2014) Phu Quoc tourism investment and development – Phu Quoc passenger port – Vietnam. http://search.proquest.com.elibrary.jcu.edu.au/docview/1617552449?accountid=16285. Accessed 11 Jan 2015

Vo Phuoc Quang Pham Mr. Vo Phuoc Quang Pham recently graduated with a bachelor's degree in Tourism and Hospitality Management from James Cook University, Australia (Singapore Campus). He currently works with Pullman Saigon Centre Hotel in Ho Chi Minh, Vietnam. His areas of research interest include hospitality, tourism development, and ecotourism.

K. Thirumaran Over the past 5 years, Dr. Thirumaran's research focus has been in Singapore, Bali, Malaysia, and Bhutan and studies on Chinese and Indian tourists. He has contributed articles in edited books, journal, encyclopedia, and newspapers. Dr. Thirumaran is a frequent guest lecturer in special interest tourism and civic education at public schools in Singapore. His teaching style provides many opportunities beyond classroom learning for students to undertake fieldwork and forge connections with the travel and hospitality industry.

Chapter 7
Optimum Stimulation Level and Shopping Experience: A Case of Australia

Tjong Budisantoso, Chun Meng Tang, Adrian Bradshaw, and Abhishek Bhati

Abstract Tourists' or regular customers' shopping behaviour is of major interest to retailers. This chapter intends to investigate the relationship between optimum stimulation level (OSL), shopping experience and retail outcome. The study is conducted in Perth, Australia; 288 shoppers participated in the study. The study found that there are significant relationships between social factors and OSL, interior layout factor and OSL, store quality and social factor and interior layout, satisfaction and store quality and repatronage intention and shopping satisfaction.

Keywords Optimum stimulation level • Store quality • Interior layout • Shopping experience

7.1 Introduction

Retail industry is very competitive, and retailers take every measure to attract tourists as well as domestic customers to their stores. However, not every customer who visits a store makes a purchase. Several studies indicate that store atmosphere has a strong influence in customer shopping behaviour. This study focuses on the physical in-store attributes which can stimulate cognitive responses of shoppers.

Retailers in Australia have invested significantly on creating an appealing store atmosphere. To maximise the outcome of this investment, an understanding of how shoppers interact with store atmosphere is needed and how store atmosphere could build shopping experience which in turn affect retail outcome. This study intends to explore the role of optimum stimulation level in interacting with the store atmosphere, how store atmosphere induces cognitive responses in terms of the perception of merchandise quality and service quality, which in turn affect store patronage satisfaction and repatronage intention. The study is conducted in Perth, Australia.

T. Budisantoso (✉) • C.M. Tang • A. Bradshaw • A. Bhati
Department of Business, James Cook University, Singapore, Singapore
e-mail: budisantoso.tjong@jcu.edu.au

P. Mandal, J. Vong (eds.), *Development of Tourism and the Hospitality Industry in Southeast Asia*, Managing the Asian Century,
DOI 10.1007/978-981-287-606-5_7

7.2 Background

7.2.1 Optimum Stimulation Level

The strength of motivation is mainly affected by the arousal level of the individual (Lawson et al. 1996, p. 318). Drive theory and expectancy theories have been used to explain the magnitude of motivation for certain behaviours (Solomon 2002, pp. 103–104). For example, drive theory argues that unfulfilled biological needs produce a tension. This tension is caused by the unpleasant state of arousal. People tend to behave to reduce this tension. Expectancy theory argues that behaviour is directed to achieve a desirable outcome.

Schiffman and Kanuk (1997, p. 99) explain that three situations can stimulate arousal needs: biological needs, emotional or cognitive processes and external stimuli in the environment. Biological needs, for example, eating or drinking, can generate arousal when these needs are not satisfied. Emotional or cognitive arousal results from thinking or daydreaming. Environment can stimulate arousal since it has collative properties such as novelty, surprise, ambiguity and uncertainty (Lawson et al. 1996, p. 319). These properties can attract people's curiosity or desire for exploration.

The literature review has covered environment congruity theories such as Berlyne's (1960) novelty-seeking approach, Fiske and Maddi's (1961) activation theory, Hunt's (1963) concept of environmental congruity, Helson's (1959), Hebb's (1955) and Leuba's (1955) optimal incongruity concepts and Driver and Streufert's (1965) general incongruity adaptation level (GIAL). Some theorists have different views on how a person explores the environment, while others have merely extended the previous concepts. Therefore, for this reason, this review explains the following theories of environment congruity briefly: those of Helson (1959), Hebb (1955), Leuba (1955), Hunt (1963) and Driver and Streufert (1965).

Hebb's (1955) and Leuba's (1955) study examined the relationship between the level of arousal and the associated cognitive response. According to their results, the cognitive response would be optimised at a moderate level of arousal produced by the cortex. The cortex can produce arousal as a result of environment incongruity. People experience a positive affect when approaching this optimum level and a negative affect when passing the optimum level.

Driver and Streufert's (1965) general incongruity adaptation level (GIAL) concept is similar in its interest in cognitive responses. Although this concept has not been supported by the empirical findings, GIAL can provide a better explanation of the relationship between the cognitive response and environmental incongruity. The adaptation level (AL) concept explains that people can have a particular adaptation level for a particular stimulus such as sound or smell. However, according to the concept of GIAL,

> Organisms could average their prior general incongruity experience over time and thus develop general expectations concerning the "normal" (consistent!) amount of general incongruity to expect in their environment. This expectation concerning general incongruity can be termed the General Incongruity Adaptation Level (GIAL). (Streufert and Streufert 1978, p. 173)

The discrepancy experienced from GIAL results in cognitive responses (Streufert and Streufert 1978, p.173). When the general incongruity in the environment is less than the GIAL value, people are motivated cognitively to explore the environment in order to approach GIAL. On the other hand, when the general incongruity in the environment is above GIAL value, people tend to reduce this incongruity through escape or perceptual distortion. Thus, people's cognitive response seeks to approach the expected value or GIAL value.

In contrast, Helson (1959) and Hunt (1963) investigate the relationship between the incongruity level and emotional or affect arousal, while McClelland (1955) and Haber (1958) introduce the concept of specific adaptation level (AL) (Streufert and Streufert 1978, p. 150). The basic assumption behind this concept is that the discrepancy between the stimuli and the AL would affect the level of emotional arousal. For example, people could have a particular adaptation level for sound or colour stimulus. To some extent, a discrepancy between the pattern of sound from the environment and the sound's AL pattern could produce a positive effect; on the other hand, a massive discrepancy could induce a negative effect.

Hunt utilises Berlyne's (1960) properties of environment, including novelty, complexity and change. These properties could arouse people when they are in the environment and stimulate the feeling of incongruity. When the incongruity increases, approaching the optimum level, the effect is positive. In contrast, when the incongruity passes the optimum level, the effect is negative. Streufert and Streufert (1978) explain that "lack of correspondence between expectancy and perception may simply have a stimulating (or pleasurable) effect, beyond this point, a disruptive (or unpleasant) effect" (p. 180).

This relationship is different to the relationship explained earlier by McClelland (1955) and Haber (1958). According to Hunt and Berlyne, the intensity of arousal declines when approaching the optimum level and increases when passing the optimum level.

Hunt, Hebb and Leuba hold different views on arousal. As is explained by Streufert and Streufert (1978), Hebb and Leuba argue that the arousal experienced by a person is produced by the cortex. This is called non-affective arousal and can influence cognitive behaviour. On the other hand, Hunt emphasises arousal induced by the environment or affective arousal.

A further concept which can explain behaviour in relation to arousal is optimum stimulation level (OSL). Optimum stimulation level refers to the way in which people's affective state responds to stimulation induced by the environment (Mittelstaedt et al. 1976; Raju 1977, 1980; Wahlers and Etzel 1985; Steenkamp and Baumgartner 1992, 1995). According to this theory, affective response follows an inverted U-shaped pattern, where the intermediate level of the curve is the optimum stimulation level. People can have either a high or low OSL. Those with a high OSL tend to pursue activities resulting in a high stimulation in order to reach the optimum level. In contrast, a low optimum stimulation person would avoid high stimulation activities. Purchasing a new product would generally be considered as a high stimulation activity (Raju 1980; Steenkamp and Baumgartner 1995).

The concept of OSL has attracted the interest of a number of consumer behaviour scholars (e.g. Raju 1977; Mittelstaedt et al. 1976; Wahlers and Etzel 1985; Steenkamp and Baumgartner 1992, 1995). Grossbart et al. (1975) find that the adoption of new retail format is influenced by OSL. However, most of the studies have identified the relationship between OSL and consumer exploratory behaviour which has been categorised by Raju (1980) as curiosity motivated, variety-seeking and risk-taking behaviours.

There are different views about the relationship between exploratory behaviour and OSL. Joachimsthaler and Lastovicka (1984, p. 833) argue that OSL does not mediate the relationship between personality traits and exploratory behaviour. In their study, OSL, social character and locus of control are found to be related to consumer exploratory behaviour. This is contrary to the view of Raju (1980). Raju (1980) found that OSL mediates the relationship between personality traits and exploratory behaviour (p. 280). The personality traits in his study are intolerance of ambiguity, rigidity and dogmatism.

Recently, Steenkamp and Burgess (2002) reconfirmed the relationship between demographics and OSL. Building on an earlier study by Raju (1980) that uncovered a relationship between age, education, working status and OSL, Steenkamp and Burgess (2002) found a relationship with gender as well (p. 146). For example, males may have a higher level of optimum stimulation than females, and young people could have a higher level of optimum stimulation than old people. In addition, OSL was found to have positive relationship with income and education.

In this study, OSL is hypothesised to be associated with store atmosphere perception and cognitive response. People who experience a high amount of arousal are likely to explore all available stimuli (Lawson et al. 1996, p. 322). Therefore, the exploration of store atmosphere is predicted to be influenced by OSL.

Lawson et al. (1996) also argue that arousal influences cognitive thinking. This influence is shown in the selection of informational stimuli and the reviewing of stored knowledge. Therefore, optimum stimulation is associated with cognitive responses, particularly the perception of merchandise quality and service quality.

7.2.2 Store Atmosphere and Cognitive Response

Studies of the influence of atmosphere in a retail context are based on the premise that the design of a retail environment could stimulate mediating responses of a physiological, emotional and cognitive nature, which may affect shopping behaviour (Bitner 1992, p. 60). This study focuses on the physical in-store attributes which can stimulate cognitive responses.

Cumulative impressions of environment can result in spatial knowledge and a personally meaningful perception which are a result of a person's interface with the environment (Schiffman and Kanuk 1997). Ittelson (1973) explains the individual predisposition to interact with the environment:

> One cannot be a subject of an environment; one can only be a participant. The environment surrounds, enfolds, engulfs and nothing and no one can be isolated and identified as standing outside of, and apart from, it. One does not, indeed cannot, observe the environment: one explores it. Environments, in addition, are always multi-modal. It may be possible to conceive of an environment which offers information through only one sense modality, but it would probably be impossible to build. (pp. 13–15)

Hence, interaction with the environment can be characterised as a multimodal learning process. This multimodal learning process affects spatial knowledge and how various aspects of spatial experience are represented in the memory (Golledge 1987; Evans and Garling 1992; Thorndyke and Hayes-Roth 1982; Taylor and Tversky 1992).

With regard to retailing, the literature reveals that store atmosphere can help to develop and facilitate the shopping experience of patrons. Kerin et al. (1992) reported that shopping experience is a result and a function of consumer interaction with the store atmosphere and the customer-related policies and practices of the store. Additionally, it is generally held that shopping experience can affect the attitudinal and behavioural responses of consumers in both retail and service sectors (p. 379).

7.2.2.1 The Classification of Store Atmosphere

While the existence of store spatial knowledge seems plausible, there are a number of distinct views about the classification of store atmosphere (e.g. Kotler 1973; Mehrabian and Russell 1974; Baker 1986; Berman and Evans 1995). Kotler (1973) defines atmosphere as "the effort to design buying environments to produce specific emotional effects in the buyer that enhance his purchase probability" (p. 50). According to this definition, store atmosphere induces emotional responses which affect purchasing decisions. The store environment is divided into (1) visual dimensions such as colour, brightness, size and shapes; (2) arousal dimensions such as volume and pitch; (3) olfactory dimensions such as scent and freshness; and (4) tactile dimensions such as softness, smoothness and temperature (p. 51).

Mehrabian and Russell (1974) divide environmental stimuli into two parts: modality variables and information rate. The purpose of this environmental stimulus classification is to measure temporal variation within each modality. The Mehrabian and Russell's (1974) model is mostly employed to explain how emotional responses influence approach-avoidance behaviour (Donovan and Rossitier 1982 and Donovan et al. 1994). The present study aims to find the relationship between the perceptions of store atmosphere and shopping behaviour; therefore, this approach cannot be utilised to achieve this aim.

A third approach to the classification of store atmosphere is that of Berman and Evans (1995). They divide the store atmosphere into (1) the exterior of the store, (2) the general interior, (3) the layout and design variables and (4) the point of purchase and decoration variables. This store atmosphere classification measures the spatial aspect of the store environment and is similar to the method used in the current study. However, the general exterior is not relevant to the present study which is interested in the store's internal variables.

This leads to the consideration of a fourth approach represented by the work of Baker (1986). Baker (1986) has developed a store atmosphere classification which consists of ambience, design and social factors. Ambience factors are background features that may or may not be consciously perceived but that affect human senses. These features include air quality, noise, scent and cleanliness. A person tolerates unpleasing ambient factors to a certain level. However, when an unpleasing environment reaches a particular level, a person consciously perceives and is affected by it (p. 81).

Design factors refer to features directly perceptible by consumers, such as aesthetics and functionality. Aesthetic design factors comprise architecture, colour, scale, materials, texture or pattern, shape, style and aesthetics. Functional design factors are layout, comfort and signage (p. 81).

Lastly, social factor refers to the people in the environment, that is, other customers and service personnel. Baker (1986) explains that the appearance, behaviour and number of people can influence the consumer's perception of the service firm. In relation to social factors, this study includes crowding as a component of the social factors (p. 81).

7.2.3 Cognitive Response

A person is at all times motivated to interact with the environment (Ittelson 1973, p. 13). The environment offers non-verbal communication for individuals (Broadbent et al. 1980; Rapoport 1982; Bitner 1992). This view is supported by Ittelson (1973) in his characterisation of environments:

> …environment always provide more information than can possibly be aroused. Environment always represents, simultaneously, instances of redundant information, of inadequate and ambiguous information, and of conflicting and contradictory information. (p.75)

Therefore, the shoppers' interaction with the store environment could result in a personally meaningful perception, influencing people's beliefs about a place, people and product (Rogers 1979; Golledge 1987; Kaplan and Kaplan 1982; Rapoport 1982).

In the retail field, the literature on store image started to emerge in 1958 when Martineau stated the idea of retail personality and defined the store image as "The way in which the store is defined in the shopper's mind, partly by its functional qualities and partly by an aura of psychological attributes" (p. 47).

Further, Kunkel and Berry (1968) explain that store image is how the image of the store is formed in the shopper's mind as the result of previous differential reinforcement (p. 22). This definition emphasises the importance of previous patronising behaviour in creating the store image.

Dichter (1985) explains that the store image is the global or overall impression of the store. Others have included attitude as part of the store image, for example,

(a) Store image is an attitude toward the store (Doyle and Fenwick 1974, p. 42)
(b) Store image is a set of attitudes based on the attributes important to the customer (James, Durand, and Dreves 1974, p. 25)
(c) Store image is a type of attitude, which is measured across a number of dimensions (Engel et al. 1986, p. 498)

The concepts of store image and store atmosphere should be differentiated (Baker et al. 1994, p. 329). Lindquist (1974) and Zimmer and Golden (1988) argue that perceptions of store atmosphere, merchandise quality and the service quality are the components of store image. However, Baker et al. (1994) find that perceptions of merchandise quality and service quality mediate the relationship between the store atmosphere and the store image. Perception of merchandise quality and service quality is the result of customer inference process (Greenberg et al. 1983, p. 152).

Mazursky and Jacoby (1986) define store image as

> a cognition and/or affect (or a set of cognitions and/or affects), which is/are inferred, either from a set of ongoing perceptions and/or memory inputs attaching to a phenomenon (i.e., either an object or event such as store, a product, a 'sale', etc.) and which represent(s) what that phenomenon signifies to an individual. (p. 147)

This definition will be utilised in this study.

While the existence of personal perceptions of retail environment seems plausible, the literature has adopted different concepts of store image development, such as attribute-based processing theory, category-based processing theory, inference theory, schema theory, the theory of affordances and the means-end chain model (see Mazursky and Jacoby 1986; Ward et al. 1992; Sirgy et al. 2000).

According to the attribute-based processing theory, the customer evaluates the store atmosphere on an attribute basis (Keaveney and Hunt 1992, p. 167). Furthermore, attributes are evaluated individually, and the final judgement is based on combining the isolated attributes (Fiske and Linville 1980; Fiske and Pavelchak 1984; Keaveney and Hunt 1992). For example, a shopper evaluates merchandise and salespeople in order to make a conclusion about the store. Keaveney and Hunt (1992) argue that the weakness of this concept is that it ignores prior experience.

The weakness of the attribute-based processing theory is addressed by the category-based processing theory (Keaveney and Hunt 1992, p. 168). According to this theory, when the buyers come to the store, they will try to compare the store environment against information stored in their memory. Specifically, they will categorise the environment according to known categories stored in their memories. If the existing category matches a memory, the relevant schema will be activated. The overall store image is a result of the schemata. When the environment does not find a match in the memory, a new subcategory will be created containing the additional information about the unique properties of the store (Keaveney and Hunt 1992).

Mazursky and Jacoby (1986) propose a model of the store image formation process. Their model consists of two basic fields: the external world or objective reality and the consumer's subjective impressions of selected elements of that world or perceived reality (p. 149). The model illustrates how the customer forms beliefs and feelings based on certain features from their reality which are congruent with their idiosyncratic cognitive configuration (p. 149). The store image is created by inferring various beliefs and feelings from perceptions. In addition to the proposed framework, Mazursky and Jacoby (1986) also explain that the store image can be characterised as having several code facets (e.g. price and merchandise information) as well as other more peripheral facets (e.g. policy and service) (p. 149).

Ward et al. (1992) introduce the theory and measurement approaches to categorisation in order to study the meaning of retail environments. According to this approach, customers categorise a retail store by comparing the attributes of a stimulus to prototypical representations of categories. The typicality of the store can be measured by the degree of similarity based on exterior and interior physical environment. Further, Ward et al. (1992) explain that the categorisation will result in prompt inferences and expectations about the categorised stimulus (pp. 127–128).

Sirgy et al. (2000) propose an integrative model of retail environment, self-congruity and retail patronage. The model can be used to analyse how shoppers match their self-concept and their ideal utilitarian store attributes with the retail images created by the retail environment. The matching process, called self-congruity, will drive retail patronage. Interestingly, the store attributes utilised include location, merchandise, price and promotion cues as parts of the retail environment beside other atmosphere cues. The means-end chain model based on the categorisation process offers a more comprehensive concept than the previous ones. Gutman (1982) defines the means-end chain as "a model that seeks to explain how a product or service selection facilitates the achievement of desired end states" (p. 60). Kerin et al. (1992) applied the model to a shopping experience study. They found that perceived store shopping experience affects the perceived value but is mediated by perceived price and quality. In addition, the perceived store shopping experience influences the perceived value directly. This finding implies three levels of abstraction: shopping experience perception (the lowest level of abstraction), perceived price and quality (a higher level of abstraction) and perceived value (the highest level of abstraction).

Other theories that support the cognitive response induced by the store environment are inference theory, schema theory and the theory of affordances (Baker et al. 2002, p. 122). Inference theory posits that people will utilise environment cues in order to make judgements of unknowns. This is supported by the theory of affordances which states that people perceive their environment as a meaningful entity. Schema theory posits that inferences about the environment are based on past experience.

The interrelation of these theories is examined in the Baker et al. (2002) study. The store atmosphere can stimulate the perception of interpersonal service quality, merchandise quality, monetary price, time or effort cost and psychic cost. These perceptions are found to relate to the perception of merchandise value. The perception of all these variables can influence behavioural intention in terms of store repatronage intention (p. 122).

The present study will focus on merchandise quality perception and interpersonal service quality perception. These perceptions are important for the consumer's decision-making (Zeithaml 1988; Kerin et al. 1992), the store image (Baker et al. 1994) and repatronage intention (Baker et al. 2002).

7.3 Research Hypothesis

In this study, OSL is hypothesised to be associated with store atmosphere perception and cognitive response. People who experience a high amount of arousal are likely to explore all available stimuli (Lawson et al. 1996). Therefore, the exploration of store atmosphere is predicted to be influenced by OSL.

H1: The perception of store atmosphere is associated with optimum stimulation level in Perth.

Bitner (1992) emphasises how store atmosphere could induce mediating responses such as cognitive, emotional and physiological responses amongst employee and customer in service context. Attribute-based process theory, category-based theory and means-end chain model support the point of view of store atmosphere-induced cognitive responses (Keaveney and Hunt 1992, p. 167). Other theories that support the point of view are inference theory, schema theory and theory of affordances. Recently, Quartier et al. (2014) found that lighting could induce shopping experience and cognitive response.

H2: Cognitive responses are associated with the perception of store atmosphere in Perth.

There is also debate in the literature about the relationship between the perception of service quality and satisfaction (Bitner and Hubbert 1994; Brady and Robertson 2001). Brady and Robertson (2001) explain that there are three ways of approaching the relationship between perceived quality and satisfaction. The first approach is that the situation or the context of the research influences the relationship between perceived quality and satisfaction (Brady and Robertson 2001). The second approach views the relationship between perceived service quality and satisfaction as "satisfaction – perceived service quality – behavioural intention". The last approach regards the relationship between perceived service quality and satisfaction as "perceived service quality – satisfaction – behavioural intention".

H3: Store patronage satisfaction is associated with cognitive responses in Perth.

Repatronage intention aims to measure the likelihood that the shopper will patronise the store in the future. This behavioural intention is the ultimate shopping outcome measurement in this study. A number of researchers (Stoel et al. 2004) argue that higher levels of satisfaction lead to repeated purchases.

H4: Repatronage intention is associated with store patronage satisfaction in Perth.

7.4 Research Method

7.4.1 The Survey

In Perth, Australia, 288 shoppers were recruited randomly to serve as subjects. The store environments chosen for the study are supermarkets, specialty stores and department stores. The number of respondents was equally distributed between types of stores. The data was collected in two shifts over 30 days at each store. The two shifts were a morning shift from 10.00 a.m. to midday and an afternoon shift from 3.00 to 5.00 p.m. It was expected that the different times and days would provide different types of shoppers: household shoppers, professionals and students. The data was collected by approaching potential respondents as they finished shopping in the store. This study used measurement instruments developed by other researchers. The main consideration in borrowing an existing measurement is that it has been established to measure particular concepts. Partial least square (PLS) is utilised to analyse the data.

7.4.2 Exploratory Factor Analysis (EFA)

The factor analysis on the OSL measurement produces two factors. The first factor represents the respondent's novelty-seeking behaviour. In contrast, the items that load most heavily on the second factor reflect a routine response. According to the concept of OSL, as defined by Steenkamp and Baumgartner (2002), the first factor more closely represents the concept of OSL. Therefore, only this factor is employed for further analysis. This factor is labelled OSL.

Factor analysis of the perception of store atmosphere measurements produces six factors. This finding is inconsistent with what the measurements intend to measure. However, the measurement results in six factors, i.e. interior design, store attractiveness, social factors, store space, aisle merchandise and crowding. These different factors may be a result of the changing store environment over the existing period. The perception of merchandise quality and service quality measurements has loaded on the same factor. This factor is labelled store quality.

The factor analysis of store patronage satisfaction has produced two factors. The first factor has most of the satisfaction concept measurements, while the second factor only comprises one measurement. Therefore, the study concentrates on the first factor. This factor is labelled store patronage satisfaction. All measurements of repatronage intention load heavily on the same factor. As a result, this factor is labelled repatronage intention.

7.4.3 Confirmatory Factor Analysis (CFA)

Measurement Model To assess the reflective measurement model, we examined internal consistency reliability (composite reliability>0.7), indicator reliability (item loading>0.7, significant at 0.05 level), convergent validity (average variance extracted (AVE) >0.5) and discriminant validity (low cross loadings on the unintended constructs and square root of the AVE are larger than the correlations between constructs) (Urbach and Ahlemann 2010). Tables 7.1 and 7.2 show the final assessment results of the reflective measurement model that were satisfactory.

Of the six factors of store atmosphere, only interior design and social factors prove to have significant relationships with store quality. Thus, the other four factors were excluded from the analysis. Also, items of respective factors that had a loading of below 0.7 were excluded from the analysis.

7.5 Structural Model Analysis

To assess the structural model, we examined R^2 (values around 0.670 are strong, 0.333 moderate and 0.190 weak), effect size (f^2 values around 0.02 are small, 0.15 medium and 0.35 large) and path coefficient in terms of sign, magnitude and significance. Figure 7.1 shows the results of the analysis: The path coefficient between OSL and social factors was significant ($\beta=0.164$, $p<0.05$, $f^2=0.027$); the path coefficient between OSL and interior design was significant ($\beta=0.16$, $p<0.01$, $f^2=0.025$); the path coefficient between social factor and store quality was significant ($\beta=0.169$, $p<0.01$, $f^2=0.07$); the path coefficient between interior design and store quality was significant ($\beta=0.461$, $p<0.01$, $f^2=0.253$); the path coefficient

Table 7.1 CR, AVE and correlations of reflective constructs

Construct	CR	AVE	OSL	Interior	Socfac	Storequa	Satis	Repatron
OSL	0.912	0.775	0.88					
Interior	0.864	0.613	0.147	0.783				
Socfac	0.945	0.896	0.155	0.536	0.946			
Storequa	0.895	0.631	0.254	0.545	0.41	0.795		
Satis	0.911	0.72	0.133	0.59	0.35	0.612	0.848	
Repatron	0.938	0.835	0.142	0.485	0.269	0.513	0.643	0.914

Note 1: *OSL* optimum stimulation level, *Interior* interior design, *Socfac* social factors, *Storequa* store quality, *Satis* store patronage satisfaction, *Repatron* repatronage intention

Note 2: *CR* composite reliability. Internal consistency reliability is satisfactory when composite reliability is above 0.7

Note 3: *AVE* average variance extracted. Convergent validity is considered satisfactory when the AVE is above 0.5

Note 4: Square roots of average variances extracted (AVE) are shown on diagonal. Correlations between constructs are shown on off-diagonal. Discriminant validity is satisfactory when square root of the AVE is larger than the correlations between constructs

Table 7.2 Factor loadings and cross loadings of reflective constructs

Items/ Construct	OSL	Interior	Socfac	Storequa	Satis	Repatron
OSL4	0.889	-0.068	0.052	-0.033	0.092	0.002
OSL5	0.889	-0.067	0.077	0.117	-0.166	0.006
OSL6	0.863	0.139	-0.133	-0.087	0.076	-0.009
Design9	-0.064	0.767	-0.144	0.021	0.056	-0.031
Ambient1	-0.035	0.838	0.235	0.094	0.051	0
Ambient2	0.092	0.744	-0.043	-0.053	-0.026	-0.003
Design6	0.013	0.78	-0.069	-0.07	-0.085	0.033
Social1	0.031	-0.087	0.946	-0.029	-0.013	0.056
Social2	-0.031	0.087	0.946	0.029	0.013	-0.056
ProdQua1	0.132	-0.028	-0.047	0.812	-0.25	0.143
ProdQua2	0.051	0.05	-0.182	0.771	-0.251	0.041
InSerQu3	0.039	0.043	-0.052	0.809	0.108	-0.036
InSerQu4	-0.091	0.025	0.143	0.832	0.149	0.023
InSerQu5	-0.138	-0.095	0.136	0.745	0.247	-0.186
Satisfa1	-0.004	-0.115	0.115	0.011	0.883	0.022
Satisfa2	-0.062	0.161	-0.137	0.053	0.853	-0.089
Satisfa3	0.1	-0.038	-0.043	-0.142	0.83	0.163
Satisfa4	-0.032	-0.005	0.062	0.076	0.826	-0.095
Repint1	0.081	0.005	0.046	-0.023	0.009	0.917
Repint2	-0.004	-0.048	-0.03	0.074	-0.086	0.918
Repint3	-0.078	0.043	-0.016	-0.052	0.077	0.906

Note 1: *OSL* optimum stimulation level, *Interior* interior design, *Socfac* social factors, *Storequa* store quality, *Satis* store patronage satisfaction, *Repatron* repatronage intention

Note 2: All item loadings are significant at 0.01 level. Indicator reliability is considered satisfactory when item loadings are >0.7, significant at 0.05 level

Note 3: Discriminant validity is considered satisfactory when items exhibit high loadings on the intended constructs (>0.5) and low cross loadings on the unintended constructs

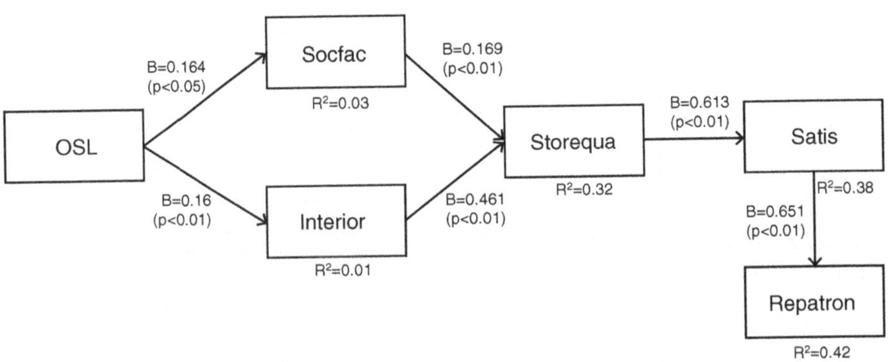

Fig. 7.1 Results of PLS analysis

between store quality and store patronage satisfaction was significant ($\beta=0.613$, $p<0.01$, $f^2=0.375$); and the path coefficient between store patronage satisfaction and repatronage intention was significant ($\beta=0.651$, $p<0.01$, $f^2=0.424$).

The construct OSL explained about 1 % of the variance of interior design and 3 % of social factor, respectively. The constructs social factor and interior design explained about 32 % of the variance of store quality. The construct store quality explained about 38 % of the variance of store patronage satisfaction. The construct store patronage satisfaction explained about 42 % of the variance of repatronage intention.

7.6 Conclusion and Future Trends

The study found partial support for the relationship between the perception of store atmosphere and OSL. Specifically, OSL is associated with the perception of interior layout and social factors in Perth, and the extent of the relationship is very low. A possible explanation is that shoppers have a high degree of familiarity with the stores. The majority of respondents (95.1 %) had visited the store before the survey was conducted. Familiarity may cause these shoppers to find most of the store atmosphere factors less stimulating. Another possible explanation is that OSL may influence how shoppers decide on their shopping goals.

This study also finds that the perception of store quality is strongly associated with that of store atmosphere. Particularly, it is associated with interior layout and social factors. Therefore, this study confirms that shoppers take their store quality cues from the store environment cues, but they do not utilise all store environment cues to form their perceptions of store quality. The study finds that shoppers give different meanings to the components of the store atmosphere in relation to the perception of store quality. Therefore, retailers in Perth should pay attention to social factors and interior layout, as these elements emerge as the most important components.

As regards the relationship between store patronage satisfaction and cognitive responses, satisfaction is strongly affected by the perception of store quality. In this study, the relationship between repatronage intention and store patronage satisfaction is confirmed. Parasuraman et al. (1988) suggest that the shoppers' evaluation of service quality could influence satisfaction. Consequently, retailers in Perth should put attention to store quality as it influences store patronage satisfaction which in turn affects repatronage intention.

While the present study contributes to our knowledge of OSL, in-store experience and retail outcome, it has several limitations. Firstly, the literature reveals that the mediating responses which are induced by store atmosphere are emotional, cognitive and physiological in nature (Bitner 1992). This study only focuses on cognitive responses, comprising the perception of merchandise quality and service quality. Secondly, as a result of using real retail settings rather than experimental ones, some factors such as pre-existing image, pre-existing emotional state and pre-existing mood could not be controlled in this study. Lastly, this study may suffer from the effect of memory recall.

References

Baker J (1986) The role of the environment in marketing services: the consumer perspective. In: Czepiel JA, Congram CA, Shanahan J (eds) The services challenge: integrating for competitive advantage. American Marketing Association, Chicago, pp 79–84
Baker J, Grewal D, Parasuraman A (1994) The influence of store environment on quality interferences and store image. J Acad Mark Sci 27:184–204
Baker J, Parasuraman A, Grewal D (2002) The influence of multiple store environment cues on perceived merchandise value and patronage intentions. J Mark 66(2):120–141
Berlyne DE (1960) Conflict, arousal and curiosity. McGraw-Hill, New York
Berman B, Evans JR (1995) Retail management: a strategic approach. Prentice Hall, Englewood Cliffs
Bitner MJ (1992) Servicescapes: the impact of physical surroundings on customers and employees. J Mark 54:57–71
Bitner MJ, Hubbert AR (1994) Encounter satisfaction versus overall satisfaction versus quality. In: Rust RT, Oliver RL (eds) Service quality: new directions in theory and practice. Sage, Thousand Oaks, pp 72–84
Brady MK, Robertson CJ (2001) Searching for a consensus on the antecedent role of service quality and satisfaction: an exploratory cross-national study. J Bus Res 51(1):53–60
Brady MK, Robertson CJ, Cronin JJ (2001) Managing behavioral intentions in diverse cultural environments: an investigation of service quality, service value and satisfaction for American and Ecuadorian fast-food customers. J Int Manag 7(2):129–149
Broadbent G, Bunt R, Jencks C (1980) Signs, symbols and architecture. Wiley, New York
Dichter E (1985) What's in an image. J Consum Mark 2(1):75–81
Donovan RJ, Rossitier JR (1982) Store atmosphere: an environmental psychology approach. J Retail 58:34–57
Donovan RJ, Rossitier JR, Marcoolyn G, Nesdale A (1994) Store atmosphere and purchasing behavior. J Retail 70:283–294
Doyle P, Fenwick I (1974) How store image affects shopping habits in grocery chains. J Retail 50:39–52
Driver MJ, Streufert S (1965) The "General Incongruity Adaptation Level" (GIAL) hypothesis: an analysis and integration of cognitive approaches to motivation. Institute for Research in the Behavioural, Economic and Management Sciences, Purdue University, Lafayette
Engel JF, Blackwell RD, Miniard PW (1986) Consumer behavior. CBS College Publishing, New York
Eroglu SA, Machleit KA (1990) An empirical study of retail crowding: antecedents and consequences. J Retail 66:201–221
Evans GW, Garling TE (1992) Environment, cognition and action: an integrated approach. Oxford University Press, New York
Fiske ST, Linville PW (1980) What does the term schema buy us? Personal Soc Psychol Bull 6:543–557
Fiske DW, Maddi S (1961) Functions of varied experience. Dorsey Press, Homewood
Fiske ST, Pavelchak MA (1984) Category-based versus piecemeal-based affective response: developments in schema-triggered affect in the handbook of motivation and cognition: foundations of social behavior. Guilford Press, New York
Golledge RG (1987) Environmental cognition. In: Stokols D, Altman I (eds) Handbook of environmental psychology. Wiley, New York, pp 131–174
Greenberg CJ, Sherman E, Schiffman LG (1983) The measurement of fashion image as a determinant of store patronage. In: Darden WR, Lusch RF (eds) Patronage behaviour and retail management. North Holland, New York
Grossbart SL, Mittelstaedt RA, Curtis WW, Rogers RD (1975) Environmental sensitivity and shopping behavior. J Bus Res 3:281–294
Gutman J (1982) A means-end chain model based on consumer categorization processes. J Mark 46:60–72

Haber RN (1958) Discrepancy from adaptation level as a source of affect. J Exp Psychol 56:370–375
Hebb DO (1955) Drives and the CNS. Psychol Rev 62:243–254
Helson H (1959) Adaptation-level theory in psychology: a study of a science. McGraw-Hill, New York
Hunt JM (1963) Motivation inherent in information processing and action. In: Harvey OJ (ed) Motivation and social interaction: cognitive determinants. Ronald Press, New York
Ittelson WH (1973) Environment and cognition. Seminar Press, New York
James DL, Durand RM, Dreves RA (1974) The use of a multi-attribute attitude in a store image study. J Retail 52:23–32
Joachimsthaler EA, Lastovicka JL (1984) Optimal stimulation level-exploratory behavior models. J Consum Res 11:830–835
Kaplan S, Kaplan R (1982) Cognition and environment. Praeger Publishers, New York
Keaveney SM, Hunt KA (1992) Conceptualization and operationalization of retail store image: a case of rival middle-level theories. J Acad Mark Sci 20(2):165–175
Kerin RA, Jain A, Howard DJ (1992) Store shopping experience and consumer price-quality-value perceptions. J Retail 68(4):376–398
Kotler P (1973) Atmospherics as a marketing tool. J Retail 49:48–64
Kunkel JH, Berry LL (1968) A behavioral conception of retail image. J Mark 32:21–27
Lawson R, Tidwell P, Raibird P, Loudon D, Della Bitta A (1996) Consumer behaviour in Australia & New Zealand. McGraw-Hill, Brisbane
Leuba C (1955) Toward some integration of learning theories: the concept of optimal stimulation. Psychol Rep 1:27–33
Lindquist JD (1974) Meaning of image: a survey of empirical and hypothetical evidence. J Retail 50(4):29–38
Martineau P (1958) The personality of the retail store. Harv Bus Rev 36:47–55
Mazursky D, Jacoby J (1986) Exploring the development of store images. J Retail 62(2):145–165
McClelland DC (1955) Studies in motivation. Appleton, New York
Mittelstaedt RA, Grossbart SL, Curtis WW, Devere SP (1976) Optimum stimulation level and the adoption decision process. J Consum Res 3:84–94
Parasuraman A, Zeithaml VA, Berry LA (1988) SERVQUAL: a multiple-item scale for measuring consumer perceptions of service quality. J Retail 64:12–37
Quartier K, Vanrie J, Cleempoel KV (2014) As real as it gets: what role does lighting have on consumer's perception of atmosphere, emotions and behaviour? J Environ Psychol 39:32–39
Raju PS (1977). Theoretical perspectives on exploratory behavior: a review and examination of their relevance to consumer research. Working paper no. 67. Working series in marketing research. Pennsylvania State University, University Park
Raju PS (1980) Optimum stimulation level: its relationship to personality, demographics, and exploratory behavior. J Consum Res 7(3):272–282
Rapoport A (1982) The meaning of the built environment. Sage Publications Inc., Beverly Hills
Schiffman LB, Kanuk W (1997) Consumer behavior. Prentice Hall, Singapore
Sirgy MJ, Grewal D, Mangleburg T (2000) Retail environment, self-congruity, and retail patronage: an integrative model and a research agenda. J Bus Res 49:127–138
Solomon MR (2002) Consumer behavior: buying, having and being. Prentice Hall, Upper Saddle River
Steenkamp JE, Baumgartner H (1992) The role of optimum stimulation level in exploratory consumer behavior. J Consum Res 19(3):434–448
Steenkamp JE, Burgess SM (2002) Optimum stimulation level and exploratory consumer behavior in an emerging consumer market. Int J Res Mark 19:131–150
Stoel L, Wickliffe V, Lee KH (2004) Attribute beliefs and spending as antecedents to shopping value. J Bus Res 57(10):1067–1073
Streufert S, Streufert SC (1978) Behavior in the complex environment. Wiley, Washington, DC
Taylor HA, Tversky B (1992) Descriptions and depictions of environments. Mem Cogn 20(5):483–496

Thorndyke PW, Hayes-Roth B (1982) Differences in spatial knowledge acquired for maps and navigation. Cogn Psychol 14(4):560–589

Urbach N, Ahlemann F (2010) Structural equation modeling in information systems research using partial least square. J Inf Technol Theory Appl 11(2):5–40

Wahlers RG, Etzel MJ (1985) Vacation preference as a manifestation of optimal stimulation and lifestyle experience. J Leis Res 17(4):283–295

Ward JC, Bitner MJ, Barnes J (1992) Measuring the prototypicality and meaning of retail environments. J Retail 68(2):194–219

Zimmer MR, Golden LL (1988) Impressions of retail stores: a content analysis of consumer images. J Retail 64(3):265–293

Tjong Budisantoso is a lecturer of marketing at James Cook University, Singapore, campus. He received International Postgraduate Research Scholarship (IPRS) from the Government of the Commonwealth of Australia in 2002. He has intensive researches in branding and retailing.

Chun Meng Tang is a lecturer at James Cook University, Singapore, campus. His major research areas include IS (information systems) evaluation, strategic IS, IS business alignment and digital innovation. He has received research grants, published journal papers, conference papers and book chapters, as well as edited various books.

Adrian Bradshaw is employed as a lecturer of business at JCU, Singapore. He has a background in computer science and physics and a career in information technology management, administration and support before attaining his PhD in management. He has a keen interest in qualitative research and the application of qualitative methods to business management, knowledge management and information systems development.

Abhishek Bhati is responsible for overseeing academic governance and administration and introducing strategies to enhance student experience for the College of Business, Law and Governance programmes offered in the Singapore campus. He has worked in the education industry with leading providers for more than 14 years. He is particularly interested in the impact of tourism on the economy as well as social sustainability. His PhD thesis studies tourist vandalism, motivation factors of a vandal's behaviour and effectiveness of stakeholder responses. His other projects include incorporating "work integrated learning" (WIL)-based learning strategies in tertiary education. His recent project involved implementing WIL in university curriculum.

Chapter 8
Understanding Dark Tourism Acceptance in Southeast Asia: The Case of WWII Sandakan–Ranau Death March, Sabah, Malaysia

Meltina Masanti

Abstract Recently, the idea of dark tourism has grown to be part of tourism fascination, and the trend has spiked to an increasing number of people traveling to visit places where battles, massacres, and evil deeds were carried out in the past. Despite the increasing demand of dark tourism visitation, Malaysia among other countries in Southeast Asia is still very careful on branding and promoting its potential attraction as "dark tourism" site. Based on the WWII Sandakan–Ranau Death March, this preliminary study is intended to understand through conceptualizing the local community acceptance toward the potential dark tourism development in Sabah, Malaysia. The study argues that due to the local community custom, belief, and culture, the exploitation of grief, death, and dark tragedy in the past as dark tourism attraction, with the intention of satisfying touristic experience, is less acceptable. It is also suggested that the acceptance factors among the local community have influenced the decision and perspective in exploring and branding a potential site as dark tourism attraction.

Keywords Dark tourism • Malaysia • Sandakan–Ranau Death March • Local community • Cultural acceptance • Southeast Asia

8.1 Introduction

> "What do you mean by dark tourism? Reliving the suffering and exhibiting the details of our grief? Some part of the past is better leave untold, let it be a history, recorded, manuscripted, but leave it like that. If everything is tourism material, what then left to our culture?" – Interview with old folks of Ranau.

M. Masanti (✉)
Tambunan Community College, Jabatan Pengajian Kolej Komuniti, Kementerian Pendidikan Tinggi Malaysia, 89650, Tambunan, Sabah, Malaysia
e-mail: meltina86@yahoo.com

P. Mandal, J. Vong (eds.), *Development of Tourism and the Hospitality Industry in Southeast Asia*, Managing the Asian Century,
DOI 10.1007/978-981-287-606-5_8

In a recent trend, dark tourism visitation is seen as a new niche of tourism attraction. Tourists have begun to look into a different dimension of touristic satisfaction and redefined the typical tourism experience. The concepts of dark tourism niche are drawing particular attention to a dark tourism site as an alternative way to enhance tourist destination toward a specific area/country. Visitors seem to be interested to visit sites where disaster, mass death, and horrifying events took place in the past. The appetite for this type of visitation interest came from people's fear of death, fear of torture and suffering, and fear of being killed. The reason why it still captivates the curiosity of certain people still remains a wide open topic for discussion. There is countless studies on the subject of dark tourism and its association to mass death, suffering as a form in tourism and hospitality fields. The term dark tourism was coined in the 1990s by John Lennon and Malcolm Foley. It describes the increasingly popular tourist practice of visiting sites associated with themes of death, dying, and atrocity (Lennon and Foley 1999). Various other terms such as "thanatourism" (Rojek 1993), "black spot" tourism (Beech 2000), and "atrocity" (Merriam-Webster 2014) are used less frequently to describe the same phenomenon.

More research focusing on the barrier development for dark tourism site attraction is still widely needed as most of the research is focusing on the motivation of visitation and few researches are available to study on the barrier of this type of visitation. It is vital to understand the motivation of this visitation in order to know the issues that contradict to the local community's beliefs and filter their administration acceptance toward the development of dark tourism. Tourism attraction development is commonly perfected with good promotion of various cultural and historical values for tourism. If dark tourism is to be developed, parties involved need to carefully understand the local community customs, belief, and culture and whether such niche of tourism development is accepted or not. While tourists may see a dark tourism site as an attempt for them to relate with death and desire to experience something that may not be morally right, the local community will react by their traditional context of religion and culture. However, this may not be same for the local community from a different ethnicity and country, for some may react openly positively, while others perceive it as negatively taboo. The objective of this study is to discuss the acceptance of dark tourism in Southeast Asia with a particular focus on the Sandakan–Ranau Death March. This will provide contextual findings and hopeful beneficial as a background framework for future research to providing more concrete and statistical data.

8.2 Background

8.2.1 Previous Studies on Dark Tourism

Dark tourism, and more specifically, genocide tourism, is defined as a travel to areas associated with death and suffering where mass deliberate and systematic destruction of a racial, political, or cultural group has occurred (Stone 2006a). Stone also mentions that there are many types of dark or macabre tourisms ranging from graveyards, celebrity death sites, fictional deaths, prisons, slavery heritage areas, and holocaust and genocide sites. Dr Stone, however, argues that the phenomenon of dark tourism has a long history, suggesting that medieval executions were an early form of dark tourism, and the practice has continued to the present day (Stone 2006b). Nowadays, the exhibition of photography, sculpture, video, and more substitutes the public witnessing of such murder, execution, and suffering. Genov agrees that dark tourism involves tourists who visit the sites of previous wars and battles, which were revived at the scene of past violence, and their tour guides cite the examples of heroism, tragedy, and personal suffering (Genov 2008). This occurs through the use of standard museological features such as the heavy dependence on the photography of atrocity. Sontag (2003), Griffith (2006), and Kleinman and Kleinman (1997) each provides a commentary on how the photography of victims produces additional distance between the victim and spectator while simultaneously objectifying the victim. Zelizer suggests that photographs, particularly of genocide and its victims, have attained an iconic status where more recent photographs mimic those of past events (Zelizer 1998).

Lennon and Foley refine the definition of dark tourism on their book titled *Dark Tourism: The Attraction of Death and Disaster*, further noting what actions do and do not constitute dark tourism. The act of friends and family visiting sites of dark tourism is not categorized as dark tourism. Conversely, "It is those who visit due to serendipity, the itinerary of tourism companies, or the merely curious who happen to be in the vicinity that are, for us, the basis of dark tourism." For the authors, it appears tourist motivations play an almost inconsequential role in dark tourism. However, in the aforementioned article, they do concede that motivations may play some role in the dark tourism experience. They quote, "These visitors may have been motivated to undertake a visit by a desire to experience the reality behind the media images and/or personal association with inhumanity" (Foley and Lennon 1996). Also discussed is that people are often thrilled and excited with new unpredictable attractions; in this case the idea of seeing something one does not see everyday fulfills the thrill seekers (Mayo and Jarvis 1981). A new destination should also offer uncertainty and complexity in order to be able to arouse a high adventure profile (Wahlers and Etzel 1985). In this modern urban age we live in, escape from boredom can often generate the inner child in us that wants to explore by selecting novel experiences (Nunnally and Leonard 1973). Repetition increases boredom, while novelty increases curiosity.

8.2.2 Southeast Asia and Its Context of Dark Tourism

Southeast Asia (SEA) is made up of 12 countries and two geographical subregions, Indochina and maritime. The Indochina zones consist of Thailand, Vietnam, Cambodia, Laos, Burma, and Peninsular Malaysia, while East Malaysia (Borneo), Indonesia, East Timor, Christmas Island, the Philippines, and Singapore are located at the maritime zones of SEA. Ethnics in Southeast Asia have their own distinct culture, customs, and belief, due to the geographical location, there are still similarities that are much more significant; these countries share similar climate and cultural trait that can be found across Southeast Asian countries (Southeast Asia: History and Geography, Livelihood (n.d.)). More to that the oceans that connected coasts and neighboring islands created smaller zones where people shared similar languages and were exposed to the same religious and cultural influences. The context of this study will try to understand the acceptance of dark tourism in Southeast Asia by comparing and also looking into the perspective case of the "Sandakan–Ranau Death March." This study will not generalize the perception of the Southeast Asian community but rather try to understand the underlying differences on culture, customs, and belief that influence attitude and acceptance toward the development of dark tourism. Historically, the religions of the Hindu, Buddhist, Islam, and Christian have shaped Southeast Asia culturally. The main religion of Indochina is prevalent throughout the region. Buddhism is predominant in the Indochinese region of SEA and Islam is predominant in the maritime zone. In the modern Indochina, Buddhism is primarily practiced with the exception of Malaysia where the official religion is Islam, while for Singapore, there is no official religion other than a diverse practice of religions.

8.3 Trend in Dark Tourism

Three of the Indochinese countries, Thailand, Vietnam, and Cambodia, are on the lead in Southeast Asia with regard to packaging sites related to past dark history as a dark tourism attraction (see Table 8.1).

Attraction sites shown in Table 8.1 are a few examples of dark tourism from its respective countries, Thailand, Cambodia, and Vietnam. Most likely the residents are able to tolerate with the dark past or thus makes them brave enough to open up or because of this niche of tourism has become increasingly popular and profitable. A visit to this niche of tourism site can turn out to be a very emotional experience, and although this niche is becoming a commonplace, dark tourism sites can be readily

Table 8.1 Established dark tourism attraction in Southeast Asia

Country	Dark tourism attraction site
Thailand	Bangkok Forensic Medicine Museum
	Songkran Niyomsane Forensic Medicine Museum, Siriraj Hospital, 2 Prannok Road, Siriraj, Bangkok Noi, Bangkok, Thailand
Cambodia	The Killing Fields, Cambodia
	Choeung Ek Killing Fields, Phnom Penh
Vietnam	Hanoi Hilton
	Hoa Lo Prison, 1 Hoa Lo St., Phu Khanh village, Hoan Kiem, Hanoi, Vietnam

Source: Author's resource

perceived as distasteful and harmful. It is hard to imagine if there is any tourist feeling joyful visiting this site and sees it as a place for a frivolous picture snapping. These sites, and many like them, are bound together by a shroud of darkness. They exemplify the darker aspects of the human experience: crime, war, death, murder, atrocity, and disaster. They also share an additional social phenomenon: tourism (Repository.tamu.edu. n.d.). By raising this type of educational awareness of the horrific past, future genocide will, hopefully, be prevented from occurring (Yuill 2003).

8.3.1 Dark Tourism in Malaysia

Although in some part of the world the visitation to a dark tourism site is becoming more common, in Malaysia, it is still unlikely to find a place that is widely promoted as a dark tourism attraction site. To date, dark tourism remains an untapped tourism product in Malaysia. Malaysia among other countries in Southeast Asia suffers a period of dark ages during the occupation of the Japanese army during WWII. Those sites, where battles, suffering, and death occurred in the past, can be developed into dark tourism product for Malaysia. Examples of possible dark tourism products are outlined in Table 8.2. Few studies have been done to explore the relationship between visitor's motivations and the host community's acceptance to such dark places in Malaysia. It's still largely unknown if the Malaysians are aware of the potential possibility of developing dark tourism site in Malaysia. Hopefully, this study will provide contextual assessment needed prior undergoing any development proposal of dark tourism. This is special between the government, the tourism industrialist, and the local community in terms of matching this perceived

Table 8.2 Potential dark tourism product in Malaysia

Potential dark tourism product in Malaysia	Locality
The WWII Sandakan–Ranau Death March	Sandakan to District of Ranau Area, Sabah, East Malaysia (Malaysia Borneo)
Penang War Museum, Malaysia	Penang, West Malaysia
Jerejak Island	Penang, West Malaysia
Pulau Bidong	Terengganu, West Malaysia
Pulau Berhala	Sandakan, Sabah, East Malaysia
Batu Lintang	Kucing, Sarawak, East Malaysia
Brothel No. 8	Sandakan, Sabah, East Malaysia
Jesselton (Kota Kinabalu)	Sabah, Malaysia, East Malaysia
Labuan	Federal Territory of Malaysia
Ranau	Sabah, East Malaysia
Pudu Prison	Kuala Lumpur, West Malaysia
Mantanani Island	Kota Belud, Sabah, East Malaysia

Source: Author's resource

expectation to influence management in the tourism setting. Further study will also strive to propose to educate managers of dark sites with regard to their knowledge on visitors' motivations and expectations and, thus, to embark guidelines on improving visitor facilities, information, and services.

Due to the lack of available information and documentation, this study is unable to find and list more potential dark tourism sites in West Malaysia. A more comprehensive research is needed to report on bigger spectrum of the potential dark tourism site around Malaysia. Referring to sites indicated in Table 8.2, some of the sites are already drawing a number of visitors to go visit the sites themselves, promoted as historical tourism sites. Except for Brothel No.8, Sandakan, and Pudu Prison, Kuala Lumpur, all others were associated with the Japanese occupation during WWII. In Malaysia, perhaps the most well-known incident was the case of WWII Sandakan–Ranau Death March, Sabah, Malaysia. By comparing to similar dark tourism sites in the world (examples include WWI battlefields – Ypres, Belgium; Auschwitz, Birkenau; Oswiecim, Poland; Old Melbourne Gaol, Melbourne, Australia; and Choeung Ek, Phnom Penh, Cambodia), the Sandakan–Ranau Death March is perhaps the most potential dark tourism site to be developed in Malaysia. The "Sandakan-–Ranau Death March" fits the description of places associated with death, whether connected to a battle and historical occurrence. The Sandakan–Ranau Death March is already drawing a large number of tourists to visit its Sandakan Memorial Park, Kundasang War Memorial Park, and Labuan War Memorial Park where all three are related to the incident. However, internationally and locally, these sites are regarded as historical sites rather than dark tourism sites.

8.3.2 The Sandakan–Ranau Death March Context

British North Borneo was administered by a Chartered Company from 1882 until January 1942 when the Japanese invaded. The largest ethnic group was Chinese, particularly Hakkas (Wong 2000). They had a pro-British disposition and had supported the British war effort through the Spitfire Fund and also sent funds to China in support of China's war against the Japanese invaders (Evans 1991). Most British were interned, initially on Berhala Island off Sandakan and, from later in 1942, in Kuching, Sarawak (Keith 1948). In July 1942, the first of two groups of Allied prisoners of war arrived from Changi in Singapore. While most of their colleagues were employed building the Burma-Siam Railway, a total of about 3,000 Australian and British prisoners of war (POWs) and 3,000 Javanese were used to build two airstrips near Sandakan on the east coast of the northern tip of Borneo. Six Australians escaped almost immediately and joined guerrilla fighters in the southern Philippines for the rest of the war or until they were killed (Richardson 1957, Wallace 1958).

Over the three years, conditions in Sandakan Prison Camp became progressively more harsh. By mid-1942, Borneo was far from the fighting and lightly garrisoned, but the surrounding waters were heavily patrolled by American submarines because of the oil routes back to Japan. As a consequence, Borneo was relatively isolated from fairly early in the war. This situation led to much anxiety and a fairly brutal style of control by the Japanese. In 1943, there was a revolt in Jesselton (now Kota Kinabalu) by the Chinese community and some Bumiputera ("native") groups (Moffat 1989). About 50 Japanese were killed and the town was held briefly before its recapture. The retributions were brutal. Entire village populations were killed and finally a group of 376 were executed at Petagas just south of Jesselton, where a large monument now marks the place.

A second insurrection at Jesselton was discovered in planning. More executions followed. Around Sandakan, an underground was established with local people and POWs (Silver 1998). Arms caches were established and radios were built. The planned insurrection was discovered in 1943. There was torture and executions of locals and POWs, and almost all the POW officers were sent to a camp at Kuching in Sarawak. From October 1944, there were regular Allied air raids on Sandakan. Rations were further reduced in the POW camp and the death rate steadily increased. By January 1945, the Japanese ceased repairing the airstrips. With this cessation of work, the rations were reduced to next to nothing (rice issues ceased). All knives and scissors were removed from the POWs. The death rate rocketed. The first death march commenced in this month. Four hundred and fifty-five of the fittest were sent on foot over a very rough trail to Ranau at the foot of Mt Kinabalu some 250km to the west. At Ranau they were worked carrying rice between Japanese bases until they died of disease and exhaustion. They died in the most appalling conditions. (As observed by Braithwaite and Lee 2006)

The Sandakan–Ranau Death March is widely known as the highlight of the Japanese army occupation in Sabah. While most of the writings are focusing only on the perspective of POWs, less known to the world is the impact of the bloody history to the people of Sabah. Referring to the oral interview conducted, the locals specially those who reside along the Sandakan–Ranau district swear of the existence of the Japanese War Tunnel. Some have been unearthed, for instance, the Japanese War Tunnel located inside the Mostyn oil palm plantation, Kunak, which belongs to Sime Darby and another one in Kudat. Due to lack of documentation and information, getting access for the purpose of investigating the other remaining Japanese occupations is difficult and time consuming. The tunnels found in Kunak are accessible, but they were not preserved properly. In fact, most of the Japanese remains in Sabah are able to keep its original structure intact whether unearthed or not, and it seems like no parties were interested in finding more of it. To what extent this is related to the local people's past suffering from the Japanese occupation is yet to be explored. Comparing with the same war tunnel outside Malaysia, for example, the Vietnam Cu Chi tunnels, the Vietnamese are taking a proactive approach and packaged the "attraction" for tourism consumption. Whether Malaysia specially Sabah is ready to take up the challenge and start to acknowledge the existence of its potential dark tourism site will depend on the acceptance spectrum of its people.

8.3.3 Cultural Acceptance of Dark Tourism

This study is not intended to investigate very sophisticated approaches on cultural acceptance but to put an insight and starting point to understanding the relationship between the cultural acceptance and tourism development – dark tourism for the context of this study. In this paper, "culture" will refer to the unique way of life of a people, including past or present, regardless of their socioeconomic status. As observed from (Shih 2003) master thesis on Cultural Acceptance and Its Effect on Tourism, Pope John Paul II (2001) addresses the importance of acceptance during his speech for the celebration of the World Day of Peace 2001:

> *The need to accept one's own culture as a structuring element of one's personality, especially in the initial stages of life, is a fact of universal experience whose importance can hardly be overestimated. Without a firm rooting in a specific 'soil,' individuals risk being subjected at a still vulnerable age to an excess of conflicting stimuli that could impair their serene and balanced development. (Para. 6)*

Some action by the local community of the country might be considered repulsive in other cultures. The judgments of outside individuals out of their cultural circle are among the major forces for culture change. The arrival of tourism also works as a tool to altered social perception. Nevertheless, the community should not be pushed to despair their cultural belief just so tourism development can make a way of it (Tables 8.3 and 8.4).

8.3.4 Cultural Acceptance Context of Dark Tourism in Sabah, Malaysia

Sabah is the home for over 31 diverse ethnic groups that live together harmoniously with each own culture, tradition, and custom being preserved. The largest indigenous group in Sabah is from the Kadazandusun tribe and lives along with the Bajau, Murut, Rungu, Lotud, Brunei, Orang Sungai, Kadayan, Bisaya, and many other subgroups. The Chinese group in Sabah forms the largest nonindigenous group. Kadazandusun is well known for their unique customs that feature female

Table 8.3 Defining culture

Attribute	Findings by previous researcher
Culture	A set of values and beliefs, norms and customs, and rules and codes that socially define a group of people, bind them to one another, and give a sense of commonality (Culture and ICC Defn OVHs W10 – De Anza College n.d.)
	"The characteristic features of a civilisation including its beliefs, its artistic and material products, and its social institutions." (Webster's New Encyclopedic Dictionary)
	"Unique bounded entities with limits and specific characteristics. Cultures were static, in that they could be captured by anthropological analyses. Their customs, habits, mores, relationships, uniquenesses could all be detailed, and in doing so, the ways in which each culture was separate from all others could be seen." (http://www.sccs.swarthmore.edu/users/00/ckennedl/culture.html) (http www sccs swarthmore edu users 00 ckennedl culture html)
	McKercher and Cros (2002) note, "Culture is not a static concept" (p. 97). As time goes on, every culture changes, sometimes imperceptibly but sometimes radically (McKercher and Cros 2002)

Source: Compiled by researcher

Table 8.4 Previous findings on cultural acceptance of dark tourism in Southeast Asia

Previous findings on cultural acceptance of dark tourism in Southeast Asia	
Cambodia	*For many Cambodians, the museums and genocide monuments are a means of preserving the country"s history, heritage and society"s collective identity. Without the money from tourists, the government would be less likely to fund the upkeep of the areas, and the memories that lie in the buildings would vanish. The sites are also used as income generation centers, which provide jobs for the locals* (Cambodia 2011)
Thailand	*"The medical museum in Bangkok "combines elements of supernatural tradition and Buddhist compassion," said Mr Algie, noting that droves of Thai schoolchildren pass through the museum each week, often leaving candy or dolls as offerings to the babies who died before childbirth"* (Dark Tourism' Creeps Out 2104)
Vietnam	*As Ho Tai (2001) explains, when examining efforts to construct cultural memories of the past, one must take into consideration "politics of memory." This creates another tension between "the uses of the past as a legitimating device and as a means of constructing community and its repackaging as a marketable commodity" (p. 6). The way in which tourism portrays Vietnam and its history plays a vital part in shaping popular memory and perception, and these tensions must be taken into consideration.* As observed from Keyes (2012)

Source: Compiled by researcher

priestesses called "bobohizan" usually to lead ancient rituals. Nowadays, most of the tribes had embraced the religion of Christianity and Islam, but some are still practicing some of their ancestral beliefs. Despite the acceptance of the religion, mostly all the local communities in Sabah, including the Chinese, are still holding on to their own custom and cultural root. Despite ethnicity and religion, the local community in Sabah has shared values and beliefs toward death, the spirit world, shamans, and deeds of respecting the deceased. In addition, their spectrum of beliefs had formed an intersection where diverse ethnic group cultural belief assimilated among them. Most of this cultural assimilation also happened because of the interracial marriage between them.

The local community of Sabah sees tragedy, death, and the open exhibition of it as taboo. Due to their diverse cultural belief and custom orders, any activity related to darkness, ghost, and tragedy is taboo and not the subject of playground. Fear on ghost and spirit world had been passed from one generation to another. Even from a young age, children had been taught with the idea of a ghost and scaring element as tools to discipline and behave them. Because of this connotation, the community avoids visiting and experiencing a place associated with darkness, death, and tragedy. Such a dark site for them is not for attraction, and one should not attempt to participate (visit) or else a tragedy, dark fate, and death follow. They also believe that attempting such place will disturb the dead spirit and "they" will follow you home. In some instances, survivors and family victims may feel uneasy toward the idea of memorializing their past death and disaster, let alone become a platform for tourism. They are also the stakeholders for the site and therefore opinion should be taken into consideration.

From what is being observed, the cultural belief of the community in Sabah has become a barrier for them into venturing to a different niche than ecotourism. It is believed that the same trait is shared with their neighboring Peninsular Malaysia where the majority of ethnic is Malay, Chinese, and Indian. Malaysia (East and West Malaysia) is culturally and religiously diverse and lives peacefully among each other. Although there is an isolated case of ethnic and racial tension, Malaysians somehow managed to emerge and were one of the most peaceful and culturally diverse countries in the world. Without generalizing that all Malaysians are superstitious but perhaps, because of their higher respect of each other's culture, customs, belief, and religion, decision that is implying a cultural impact is sensitive. The output of this study conceptualizes the context without discussing the complexity of definition, previous suggested framework, and statistical evidence (Fig. 8.1).

Therefore, this study suggests that Malaysia through the cultural integration had formed a version of "Culture of Malaysia." The concept somehow represents the ideal culture for Malaysia, without compromising the ethnic group cultural belief and stepping the boundaries of religion. With sensitivity and respect as a keyword, this ideal "culture" will anticipate in further development of tourism. Perhaps, this is what differentiates Malaysia from the rest of its neighboring Southeast Asian country that is already in the lead of promoting and branding their dark site and war site as dark tourism. Although with vast prospect of dark tourism site in Malaysia like the Sandakan–Ranau Death March, cultural acceptance is still a pivotal aspect of assessment. As suggested in the abstract, local community custom, belief, and culture, the exploitation of grief, death, and dark tragedy in the past with the intention of satisfying touristic experience is less acceptable and remains uncommon. It also suggested that the cultural acceptance factors among the local community have influenced the decision and perspective in exploring and branding potential site as

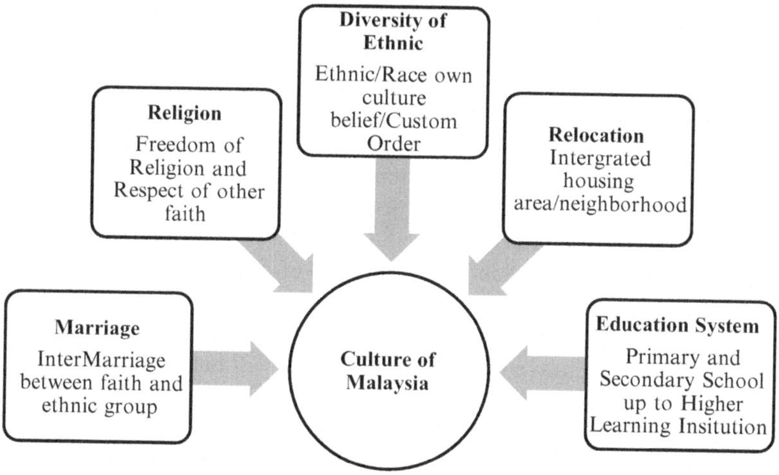

Fig. 8.1 Suggested framework of culture integration in Malaysia (Source: suggested by researcher)

dark tourism attraction. Hopefully, future research will be able to provide more statistical and concrete evidence to support these findings.

8.4 Future Trends

The demand of "dark tourism" is now getting more attention from audience worldwide; thus, it is timely a call for the government and industry to come out with an ideal development plan to please that demand. Research on a better understanding with regard to the creation of supply infrastructure to the emerging trend is vital. Addressing the conflict of interest between society cultural acceptance, religious view, and custom and belief toward the potential place of interest on dark tourism should be made priority before the industry can determine the accessibility of a place. In the meantime, the local community needs to be educated carefully on preserving those past monument, places, and tragedy. The approach should be varied depending on each community's cultural ties and values. The local community needs to be taught on moving on from the past event and validate the tragedies as a lesson to learn and share.

8.5 Conclusion

Although the possibility to establish a dark tourism product/site is culturally sensitive for the local community in Sabah and Malaysia, the potential to tap dark tourism as an additional tourism revenue product in Sabah is still possible. This can be done if the dark tourism product is marketed in appropriate manner without excessively touching the sensitivity of the local community. Perhaps, their custom, belief, and cultural order and superstitious belief on the spirit world can be packaged together with dark tourism – then producing "a better" own version of dark tourism, where tourists visit to commemorate site and operators can exhibit death, grief, and suffering without stepping the cultural boundaries of local community. Studying the cultural acceptance of dark tourism in Southeast Asia, Malaysia, and context of Sandakan–Ranau Death March helps to understand how dark tourism can be developed, managed, and presented and the right marketing strategies for Malaysia and the international market. Government and tourism industrial player should start building assessment framework and development strategies for the potential dark tourism sites. Venturing into a new niche of tourism will help to sustain Malaysia's eco-tourism related sources like the mountain, rainforest, diving site from being overused by tourism industry. This can be done by diverting their interest and providing a different alternative for their visitation here. Although the typology and motivation of visiting vary among tourists, continuous promotion and support from the local community will help add dimension on the perception of tourism product in Malaysia.

References

Beech J (2000) The Enigma of Holocaust sites as tourist attractions – the case of Buchenwald. Manag Leisure 5:29–41

Braithwaite D, Yun L (2006) Dark tourism, hate and reconciliation: the Sandakan experience. International Institute for Peace through Tourism (IIPT), No. 8

Culture and ICC Defn OVHs W10 – De Anza College (n.d.) Retrieved from http://facultyfiles.deanza.edu/gems/khannaanu/CmuCultureDefn.pdf

Dark Tourism' Creeps Out Thailand (2104, July 23) Retrieved September 16, 2014, from http://www.bangkokpost.com/news/local/421943/dark-tourism-creeps-out-thailand

Foley M, Lennon J (1996) JFK and dark tourism: a fascination with assassination. Int J Heritage Stud 2:198–211

Genov G (2008) Special interest tourism (Turizam posebnih interesa), pp 13–15, 169–172. Cigura print, Belgrade

Griffith D (2006) A good war is hard to find: the art of violence in America. Soft Skull Press, New York

http://www.sccs.swarthmore.edu/users/00/ckenned1/culture.html

Introduction to Southeast Asia: History, Geography, and Livelihood (n.d.) Retrieved September 18, 2014.

Keyes M (2012) War tourism: shaping memory and perception in post-war Vietnam. University of Puget Sound Sound Ideas Summer Research, 164–164. Retrieved August 16, 2014

Kleinman A, Kleinman J (1997) The appeal of experience; The dismay of images: cultural appropriation of suffering in our times. In: Das V, Kleinman A, Lock M (eds) Social suffering. California: University of California Press, pp. 1–23

Lennon JJ, Foley M (1999) Interpretation of the unimaginable. The U.S. Holocaust Museum, Washington

Mayo E, Jarvis LP (1981) The psychology of leisure travel. CBI Publishing Co., Boston

McKercher B, Cros H (2002) Cultural tourism. The Haworth Hospitality Press, New York

Merriam-Webster (2014) Genocide. Retrieved from http://www.merriamwebster.com/dictionary/genocide

Nunnally JC, Leonard LC (1973) Exploratory behavior and human development. Adv Child Dev Behav 8:59–109

Repository.tamu.edu. (n.d.). Retrieved from http://repository.tamu.edu/bitstream/handle/1969.1/89/etd-tamu-2003C-RPTS-Yuill-1.pdf.txt?sequence

Rojek C (1993) Ways of seeing-modern transformations in leisure and travel. Macmillan, London

Shih I (2003) Cultural acceptance and its effect on tourism. University of Nevada, Las Vegas

Sontag S (2003) Regarding the pain of others. Picador Press, New York. DC J Travel Res 38:46–50. Stone PR (2006) A dark tourism spectrum: towards a typology of death and macabre related tourist sites, attractions and exhibitions. Tourism 54(2):145–160.

Stone PR (2006a) A dark tourism spectrum: towards a typology of death and macabre related tourist sites, attractions and exhibitions. Tourism 54(2):145–160

Stone D (2006b) History, memory and mass atrocity: essays on the Holocaust and genocide. Valentine Mitchell Publishers, London

Trend Analysis: Genocide Tourism in Cambodia (2011) Trend analysis: genocide tourism in Cambodia. Retrieved September 18, 2104, from https://atrium.lib.uoguelph.ca/

Wahlers RG, Etzel MJ (1985) Vacation preferences as a manifestation of optimal stimulation and lifestyle experience. J Leisure Res 17:283–295

Webster's New Encyclopaedic Dictionary, p. 244

Yuill SM (2003) Dark tourism: understanding visitor motivation at sites of death and disaster. Informally published manuscript, Department of Science, Texas A&M University, Education City, Qatar, Texas

Zelizer B (1998) Remembering to forget: Holocaust memory through the Camera's Eye. Chicago University Press, Chicago

Meltina Masanti Meltina Masanti previously works as a Polytechnic's lecturer at Sandakan Polytechnic, and attached with the Department of Tourism and Hospitality. Her areas of research interest include Dark Tourism, Community Based Tourism in Borneo, South East Asia Hospitality Industry and Tourism Development.

Index

P. Mandal, J. Vong (eds.), *Development of Tourism and the Hospitality Industry in Southeast Asia*, Managing the Asian Century,
DOI 10.1007/978-981-287-606-5

The manufacturer's authorised representative in the EU is Springer Nature Customer Service Centre GmbH, Europaplatz 3, 69115 Heidelberg, Germany. If you have any concerns regarding our products, please contact ProductSafety@springernature.com

Printed and bound by CPI Group (UK) Ltd, Croydon, CR0 4YY
22/09/2026
02220945-0019